Call to Holiness

Reflections on the
Catholic Charismatic Renewal

Most Reverend Paul Josef Cordes

Foreword by
Reverend Raniero Cantalamessa, O.F.M. Cap.

A Michael Glazier Book

The Liturgical Press   Collegeville, Minnesota

A Michael Glazier Book published by The Liturgical Press

Design by Frank Kacmarcik, Obl.S.B.

Cover illustration by the Spanish painter KIKO ARGUELLO. Depicting Pentecost, it is a copy of a fresco found in a Church in Florence, Italy. In conformity with an iconographic tradition, the royal figure represents the universe and indicates that from Pentecost the announcement of the Gospel stretches throughout the universe.

Excerpts from paragraphs 739, 772, 792, 800, 801, 890, 1212, 1504, 1508, 1509, 2035 and 2013–17 from the English translations of the *Catechism of the Catholic Church* for the United States of America, copyright © 1994, United States Catholic Conference, Inc.—Libreria Editrice Vaticana.

2	3	4	5	6	7	8

Library of Congress Cataloging-in-Publication Data

Cordes, Paul Josef.
    Call to holiness : reflections on the Catholic charismatic renewal
/ Paul Josef Cordes : foreword by Raniero Cantalamessa.
      p. cm.
    "A Michael Glazier book."
    Includes bibliographical references.
    ISBN 0-8146-5887-3 (alk. paper)
    1. Pentecostalism—Catholic Church.   2. Catholic Church—
Membership.   3. Catholic Church—Doctrines—History—
20th century.
    I. Title.
BX2350.57.C68   1997
269'.088'22—dc21   97-37799
                                                        CIP

CONTENTS

FOREWORD

Beginning with the phenomenon of the Montanists of the second century, the history of the Church records diverse prophetic and charismatic movements. The majority of these, after a period of intense and spectacular growth, have ended up on the fringes of the Church or completely lost. One of the primary reasons for this is the fact that they immediately enter into conflict with the institutional and hierarchical elements of the Church. Today, some question whether in certain instances this could not have been avoided to the great benefit and richness of Christian life if such movements had been guided more attentively and given a better welcome by the rest of the Church.

From this perspective one is struck so often by the novelty represented by the Charismatic Renewal. From the time of the Renewal's beginning in the Catholic Church in 1967, not so long ago, it appears to have been inspired by a profound attachment and love of the institutional Church and to her qualified representatives: the Holy Father, the bishops, and the priests. This was what most favorably impressed me when coming in contact with the reality of the Renewal for the first time.

The primary credit for this is not however due to the Charismatic Renewal, rather to the hierarchy. With an almost miraculous security, the hierarchy has recognized this reality of the Renewal, since its beginnings, as its own and as a genuine work of the Spirit, despite the new and unusual characteristics it presented. The prophetic intuition of Pope Paul VI had a determining role in this, in that, on Pentecost of 1975 at a meeting with its leaders, he defined the Charismatic Renewal as a "chance" for the Church. Since then interventions by the popes have increased (cf. K. McDonnell, *Open the Windows. The Popes and the Charismatic Renewal*, South Bend, Indiana, 1989); not to mention documents published by individual bishops or by episcopal conferences, or by the leaders of other Christian denominations (three volumes written before 1980 and edited by the same author under the title *Presence, Power and Praise*, The Liturgical Press, Collegeville, Minnesota, 1980).

An evolving series of these interventions is composed of the so-called "Documents of Malines," in which the late L. J. Cardinal Suenens, designated by Pope Paul VI as his representative to the movement, gave direction on specific points of the Charismatic Renewal. What renders these documents particularly significant is that they are, at the same time, fruits of the discernment of the Magisterium as well as of a knowledge and direct participation in the Charismatic phenomenon.

The present document by Archbishop Paul Josef Cordes, the successor of Cardinal Suenens as "Episcopal Adviser" to the Charismatic Renewal, may be introduced into this sequence. Archbishop Cordes, who served for more than ten years as a guide for the Charismatic Renewal, was doctrinally attentive and enlightened, while at the same time a fraternal and encouraging presence. Thanks to his discreet and silent work, he was able to make important strides in efforts to pass from the fringes to the very heart of the Catholic Church. Pontifical approval given to the "Catholic Fraternity of Covenant Communities and Fellowships" in 1990 and to the Statutes of the Representative Office of the "International Catholic Charismatic Renewal" in 1993 marked significant moments along this journey.

In leaving this assignment as "Episcopal Adviser" to take up that of the Presidency of the Pontifical Council "Cor Unum," Archbishop Cordes thought to offer us this contribution, fruit of his experience, dialogue, and study. The central points that are examined in this text are three: "Baptism in the Spirit," charisms, and ecumenism.

In developing each one of these points, a strong but delicate balance is noted in the application of the principles of theological and spiritual discernment, matured from the secular wisdom of the Church, to the new reality of the Charismatic Renewal. I am convinced that the text will be of great use, not only to the members of the Charismatic Renewal and most of all to its leaders, but also to the rest of the Church and in particular, to pastors. All of these will find in this text a first-hand synthesis that will immensely facilitate their task of understanding and valuing this reality that Cardinal Suenens defined as "a current of grace destined to all the Church."

Archbishop Cordes returns to the theme of ecumenism, already the subject of one of the documents of Malines. He is right in doing so, since ecumenism in the interim has covered new ground and brought to light new problems. His Excellency insists in placing us on guard about certain drawbacks that can derive from a practice of ecumenism not sufficiently enlightened. His intention is repeated several times. However, it is not to discourage engagement in this effort toward unity, but to preserve that which has been, in its origin, one of the most evident blessings of the Charismatic Renewal.

The task of the Charismatic Renewal in this sector is certainly not to replace doctrinal and official dialogue among Christian Churches or to ignore it. Rather the task is to journey alongside and support this dialogue with the ecumenism of mutual knowledge and love. In his Apostolic Letter *Tertio millennio adveniente,* Pope John Paul II presents unity between Christians as one of the principal or main objectives of the Great Jubilee of the Year 2000 and desires that this Year 2000 be "a promising opportunity for fruitful cooperation in the many areas which unite us; these are unquestionably more numerous than those which divide us" (no. 16). It is in this direction that, with the help of this text, the Charismatic Renewal can give, and I believe has already given, its specific contribution to this commitment defined as "irreversible." That is the commitment of the Catholic Church for the unity of Christians.

I can only encourage all those interested to take into their hands this precious instrument of spiritual discernment. I would like to thank Archbishop Cordes for this and for the numerous other signs of goodwill and friendship he has demonstrated toward the Charismatic Renewal and other ecclesial movements inspired by the Spirit in the Church after the Council. I do this purely on a personal level, having no other reason to do so. At the same time, I believe that I express the feelings of all in the Catholic Charismatic Renewal.

Fr. Raniero Cantalamessa, O.F.M. Cap.

INTRODUCTION

The Pentecostal Movement is considered to be "the fastest grow-ing missionary movement in the world." It is multiplying at a unique rate. "A growth from zero to four hundred million in ninety years has never before been experienced in the entire history of the Church."[1] The sober observer of the present situation in the Church may dismiss such a statement as triumphalist trumpet blowing against the institution or as a warning cry of conservatives. The fact is: The "Pentecostal Movement" is a theological and pastoral chal-lenge of the present day. Neither suppressing nor ignoring this will do justice to the fact. This faith phenomenon deserves as few others our interest, especially that of the shepherds of the Church and their co-workers.

Among the first to understand this need was the now deceased Cardinal of Malines-Brussels, His Eminence L. J. Cardinal Suenens. Through years of participation in meetings on the world level and numerous visits to its various centers, he came to know the Movement and the inherent power, which was the source of its suc-cess. In a certain sense he opened for it the gates of St. Peter.

On the Feast of Pentecost in the Holy Year 1975, twenty-five thou-sand pilgrims celebrated the Eucharist together with Pope Paul VI on the grave of the Apostle. Approximately ten thousand of them were representatives of the Charismatic Renewal. The Holy Father embraced the Cardinal from Brussels at the "Confessio" with the words: "I thank you, not in my name, but in the name of the Lord, for what you are doing and will do, to lead the Charismatic

---

[1] W. J. Hollwenweger, "From Azusa Street to the Toronto Phenomenon: Historical Roots of the Pentecostal Movement," *Pentecostal Movements as an Ecumenical Challenge* (ed. J. Moltmann and K. J. Kuschel) in *Concilium* (1996/3) 3–14.

Renewal into the heart of the Church."[2] Later the pastoral care for the Movement was officially confirmed when the Pope named the Cardinal "Episcopal Adviser" for the Renewal.

Cardinal Suenens wrote a series of theological studies in which he pointedly addressed central questions and problems facing the Renewal. He developed these—as he describes in his autobiography—in conjunction with an international group of theologians, in order to assure the needed credibility for the Movement and, on the other hand, to defend it from possible errors or disdain. Since neither theological reflection nor pastoral planning is the basic intent of the Renewal, it needs the indispensable guidance of the Church and its Teaching Office. No one can possibly wish that the true freedom of the spirit should be replaced by self-seeking independence (cf. Gal 5:13) or that the unity of the Church should be destroyed by rivalries and cliques (cf. 1 Cor 4:7). Cardinal Suenens writes: "I wish to achieve with these writings what every bishop is commissioned to do at his consecration: 'Ut evellat et destruat, ut aedificet et plantet'—that he may root out and destroy, that he may build up and plant."[3]

At the beginning of 1984 Cardinal Suenens requested Pope John Paul II to release him from his responsibility of being "Episcopal Adviser" for the Renewal, and to place this burden on other shoulders. In a letter of May 23, 1984, His Eminence A. Cardinal Casaroli, the then Cardinal Secretary of State, informed me that the reasons given by Cardinal Suenens had been taken into consideration and the Congregation for the Doctrine of the Faith, which had accompanied the Charismatic Movement from the beginning had been consulted. The result of these consultations led to the wish of Pope John Paul II that I should take over the responsibilities of "Episcopal Adviser" from Cardinal Suenens.

Until December 1995, when I was named President of the Pontifical Council "Cor Unum," I have done my best within the scope of my possibilities to fulfill this responsibility—through participation in larger international meetings, through visits to

---

[2] Léon-Joseph Cardinal Suenens, *Memoirs and Hopes* (Dublin: Veritas, 1992) 291.
[3] *Ibid.*, 279.

various Charismatic communities and groups, through participation in committees and consultative bodies on the world level, and through contacts with individual charismatic leaders—by way of critique and encouragement.

Early on I had the idea of resuming the intellectual and spiritual guidance of the "Renewal," which Cardinal Suenens had begun in the "Malines Documents." The theological implications of the lived spirituality of the Renewal—as is the case of every living thing—is undergoing change; the process cannot be considered as completed. On the contrary, spirituality, which is the "subjective side of dogmatics" (H.U. von Balthasar), needs continued dialogue with a definitive theology—not in order to "domesticate" faith life, but to keep it bound to the truth which God proclaims in Revelation and the Teaching of the Church. It is characteristic of all new breakthroughs—including those in the spiritual realm—that the importance of experience and testimony for everyday life and for the apostolate is greater than that of specific articles of faith and theological reflection. Nevertheless the noteworthy fruits of the "lived testimony" (cf. 1 Pet 2:12) should not detract from the fact that faith also has a rational dimension, that can only arrive at certainty through an earnest process of verification. When fortunately, on the one hand, the Charismatic Renewal shows through its apostolic dedication the limitations of Rationalism, so on the other hand, it is also necessary that it avoids the extremes of blind *fideismus* or emotional bliss.

Therefore, it is important to again consider certain terms, which are characteristic for this Movement, terms such as "experience" or "Baptism in the Holy Spirit." Typical charisms such as "inner" or "external healing" or the concept of "prophecy" need to be reevaluated in order to protect them from false interpretation or misunderstanding. In the prayer groups and communities there have developed tried and tested forms of communal life. What is their relationship to the structures of the local Church? Finally, thought must also be given to the ecumenical contacts between Catholic and non-Catholic groups in the Charismatic Renewal. The origins of this Movement demonstrate a special responsibility toward Jesus' prayer for unity. From this it cannot be understood that an individual Charismatic or Charismatic group can abandon the Catholic Church, forming with non-Catholic Charismatics a "Charismatic denomination" which would anticipate "in the Spirit" the unity of all the baptized. This would be a false development, which would not only lead to a new division of Christians, but would also gamble away the true calling of the Charismatic Renewal within the Church.

Beyond the indispensable pastoral care of individual shepherds, many local Churches and national conferences of bishops have in the interim made statements regarding the concrete questions which the Charismatic Renewal raises. Still, on the international level as well, a theological orientation and pastoral care appeared to be desirable.

The first impulses in this direction came out of a conference of representatives of the movement, which I called together in Rome several years ago. These representatives pointed out especially three pastoral problems: the exodus from the Church of many Catholic Christians who had been touched by the Charismatic Renewal; resistance or even rejection of the Renewal by Church authorities and parish groups; and the often apathetic willingness within the Charismatic Renewal to surrender those specific characteristics which identify Charismatic spirituality. Two concrete preemptive measures to address these dangers of the true charisma of the Renewal have been in the interim completed: the papal recognition on November 11, 1990, of the Catholic Fraternity of Charismatic Convenant Communities and Fellowships as a private association of the faithful and the papal confirmation on September 14, 1993, of the Statutes of the International Catholic Charismatic Renewal Services.

The considerations, which are presented in the present work, *Call to Holiness: Reflections on the Catholic Charismatic Renewal,* are intended as a further step in preserving and increasing the fruitfulness of the special charism of the Charismatic Renewal for the Catholic Church and for the unity of Christians. They are nothing more than an on-going theological and pastoral contribution to the Renewal. The text has a long history and brings with it an abundance of comments and statements by responsible persons, both lay and theologians, who know the movements as insiders. Several of these I want to specifically mention: Nikol Baldacchino, Malta; Hans Gasper, Germany; Kim Catherine-Marie Kollins, Germany; Ralph Martin, U.S.A.; Fr. Fio Mascarenhas S.J., India; Fr. Ken Metz, U.S.A.; Brian Smith, Australia; Charles Whitehead, England.

Two bishops, who are not specifically a part of the movement, were also consulted: Most Reverend Eugenio Corecco, the now deceased Bishop of Lugano, and Most Reverend Ricardo Blázques Pérez, Bishop of Bilbao and Chairman of the Theological Commission of the Spanish Conference of Bishops.

Two co-workers whom I want especially to thank, because without their help the present final edition of this text would not have come about, are: Fr. William Thomas (Knetzgau, Germany; that is, Lansing, Michigan, U.S.A.) and Fr. Kilian McDonnell O.S.B. (Collegeville, Minnesota, U.S.A.).

A new evangelization needs its messengers. In light of the enormous challenge of secular society and the preparation for the Great Jubilee of the Year 2000, Pope John Paul II is seeking to recruit additional witnesses for the proclamation of salvation in Jesus Christ. He is counting no less on the new spiritual movements in the Church. On the Vigil of Pentecost 1996, he pointed to the importance of this day for the mission of the Church:

"One of the Spirit's gifts to our age is certainly the flowering of ecclesial movements, which from the very beginning of my Pontificate I have continued to identify as a reason for hope for the Church and for mankind. They are 'a sign of the freedom of forms in which the one Church is realized, and they represent a sound innovation which still wants to be adequately understood in full and positive effectiveness for the kingdom of God, working at this moment in history' (*Insegnamenti*, VII/2 [1984], p. 696). In the framework of the celebrations of the Great Jubilee, especially that of the year 1998, dedicated in a particular way to the Holy Spirit and his sanctifying presence within the community of Christ's disciples (cf. *Tertio millennio adveniente*, no. 44), I am counting on the joint witness and the collaboration of the movements. I am confident that, in communion with the pastors and linked with diocesan programs, they will want to bring their spiritual, educational and missionary riches to the heart of the Church as a precious experience and proposal of Christian life."[4]

Archbishop Paul Josef Cordes

[4] Pope John Paul II, Homily on the Vigil of Pentecost, May 25, 1996, *L'Osservatore Romano*, English ed., no. 22; May 29, 1996.

CHAPTER 1

THE SPIRITUAL RENEWAL COMING FROM THE COUNCIL

Among the many themes that emerged during the Vatican Council two have special importance in the present context: the call to holiness and mission. Pope John Paul II has repeatedly returned to these topics, indicating deep urgency. In the tradition of Pope Paul VI, as expressed in *On Evangelization in the Modern World*, the present Pope has also stressed the personal moment in faith, the personal encounter with the Lord, as essential to evangelizing and re-evangelizing the world. Holiness, mission, and the personal moment in faith are not new mandates, but are the gifts of baptism.

When Jesus is heard saying "Be perfect as your heavenly Father is perfect" (Matt 5:48) many are discouraged because they misunderstand the nature of holiness, thinking it primarily the result of personal asceticism. On the contrary, it is first of all a free, unmerited gift. "The love of God has been poured into our hearts through the Holy Spirit that has been given us" (Rom 5:5). We are invited to be perfect as the heavenly Father is perfect because we carry within us that life of the Father given through Christ in the Spirit, given without cost to us. We start at the top of the ladder, not at the bottom.[1]

Since in celebrating the Sacraments, especially Baptism, we participate in the mysteries of Christ's passion, death, and resurrection; we have communion in the very life of God. "I am the vine, you are the branches" (John 15:5). One and the same life in the vine and the branches. Again, if Christ is the head of His body, the Church, no other life is in the members of the Church, but the life of the head. One and the same life in head and members.

[1] Karl Adam used this image in his lectures in Tübingen.

This involves us in a trinitarian drama, a trinitarian journey. The holiness God has, God has absolutely, without decision, without limit, by virtue of the divine nature. The holiness we have is by communion in the divine holiness, not by virtue of our own identity, but by participation in what is God's. The Father reaches through the Son in the Spirit to touch the Church, endow it with divine life, transform it, and lead it in the Spirit, through Christ, back to the Father. One and the same life in the Trinity and in us. One and the same holiness in the Trinity and in us.

The Spirit is the power of life in the Church and the world. What the Spirit touches, the Spirit changes. As St. Ephrem indicates, this is the divine plan in the incarnation, Jesus' own Baptism in the Jordan, our Baptism, and the Eucharist: "Fire and Spirit are in the womb of her who bore You, Fire and Spirit are in the river in which You were baptized, Fire and Spirit are in our baptism, and in the Bread and Cup is Fire and the Holy Spirit."[2]

Holiness is communion in the rhythms of this going out from the Father and returning to the Father by means of the Spirit and the Son, the two hands of God, in St. Irenaeus' famous phrase.[3] To be a saint is to let shine forth this rhythm of divine life given without cost to us: "Become holy yourselves in every aspect of your conduct, after the likeness of the holy One who called you" (1 Pet 1:15). To be a saint is to respond with adoration and awe, penance and asceticism to the initiative the Father takes—an initiative the Father maintains at every point in the progress back to the absolute start, the Father. Saints are those who "hold on to and perfect in their lives that sanctification which they have received from God" (LG 40). Once again, we start at the top of the ladder, not at the bottom.

Here is the inalienable basis of Christian joy, the indestructible ground of Christian optimism. "Neither death, nor life, nor angels, nor rulers, nor things present, nor things to come, nor powers, nor height, nor depth, nor anything else in all creation, will be able to separate us from the love of God in Christ Jesus our Lord" (Rom 8:38-39).

---

[2] *Hymns on Faith* 10:17; *Corpus Scriptorum Christianorum Orientalium* 155:35–36.
[3] *Against Heresies* 4,20,3; SCh 100:632.

The angel of the Lord told Mary that when the Holy Spirit over-shadowed her "the child to be born will be holy; he will be called Son of God" (Luke 1:35). The Spirit who is given in this mystery is given without measure. What Jesus is by nature, we are by adoption, by participation, by grace. When the Spirit comes down upon us at Baptism, we become sons and daughters of God, living the same life. To us the Spirit is given in measure, but also in abundance, pressed down and overflowing. But one divine life, one divine holiness in God and in us. Indeed, so central is this sharing in the divine life and holiness that for St. Athanasius it sums up the whole purpose of the Incarnation: "The Son of God became the Son of man in order that the sons of men, the sons of Adam, might be made sons of God."[4] Being children of God they receive the seed of the resurrection and immortality.

No mistake should be made about this call to holiness. The Council is emphatic: "All the faithful of Christ of whatever rank or status are called to the fullness of the Christian life and the perfection of charity" (*LG* 40). The laity and clergy both are called to the heights of holiness, without distinction. And it is the same holiness: "One and the same holiness is cultivated by all who are moved by the Spirit of God, and who obey the voice of the Father, worshiping the Father in spirit and truth" (*LG* 41).

When the Spirit came down on Jesus at His Baptism in the Jordan it was ordered to proclaim "the good news to the poor" (Luke 4:18). Our communion with the Spirit in our Baptism contains the mandate to evangelize. This is not an option but an imperative. There can be no true vertical communion in the Spirit through Christ if there is not a horizontal communion with our neighbor through sharing the wealth of the Gospel (cf. 1 John 4:9-21). What is true of the Apostle Paul is true of every baptized person: "Woe to me if I do not proclaim the gospel" (1 Cor 9:16). Further, if there is a communion from above (Spirit, Christ, Trinity, Eucharist) into which we enter without payment, there must be a corresponding communion from below of earthly wealth (sharing of food, educational opportunities, the restructuring of the social order, etc.). As Pope Paul VI said, the social dimensions of the Gospel are not "foreign to evangelization."[5]

[4] *On the Incarnation. Against the Arians* 8; *PG* 26:997.
[5] *On Evangelization* 30, *AAS* 68 (1976) 25–26.

As the twentieth century draws to a close and the twenty-first appears on the horizon, the Spirit stirs again in the Church, implanting in hearts a desire for holiness in all of its amplitude. The desire for the heights of holiness is already the beginning of holiness. "Yearning makes the heart deep."[6] This stirring of the Spirit in the life of the Church manifests itself in a renewed interest in prayer, in new forms of community life, in several and different new ecclesial movements, in new forms of social outreach.

Prophetically, Pope Paul VI foresaw this fresh springtime in the Church. He said that "the Church has felt as though the Spirit of Christ were flowing back within her . . . ."[7] And again: "We live in the Church at a privileged moment of the Spirit."[8] Only one of the signs of recovery of Pentecost as a permanent part of the Church's life is the Charismatic Renewal or Renewal in the Spirit. Pope John Paul II has confirmed that "the vigor and the fruits of the Renewal certainly testify to the powerful presence of the Holy Spirit in the Church during these years following the Second Vatican Council . . . . The Charismatic Renewal is an eloquent manifestation of this vitality today, a vigorous affirmation of what 'the Spirit is saying to the Churches' (Rev 2:7) as we draw near to the end of the second millennium."[9]

The Charismatic Renewal has been described as an experiential discovery of the power of the Holy Spirit in the Church and in her individual members. This demands theological and pastoral reflections so that the Renewal may remain vital in the heart of the Church. The mercy God has shown the Charismatic Renewal is that which precedes and accompanies all the works of God. We bow down in wonder. "Blessed be the God and Father of our Lord Jesus Christ, who has blessed us in Christ with every spiritual blessing in heavenly places, just as he chose us in Christ before the foundation of the world to be holy and blameless before him in love" (Eph 1:3-4).

---

[6] Augustine, *Tracts on the Gospel of John* 40:10; *CC* 36:356,5.

[7] Christmas Message of 1965.

[8] *On Evangelization* 75, *AAS* 68 (1976) 64–67.

[9] Address to the Sixth International Assembly of the Charismatic Renewal, May 15, 1987.

CHAPTER 2

THE EXPERIENCE OF
THE HOLY SPIRIT AND ITS FRUITS

2.1. "Baptism in the Holy Spirit"

There are various possible approaches to an understanding of the Charismatic Renewal. From the perspective of salvation history, the link to the descent of the Holy Spirit in Jerusalem on Pentecost becomes evident. This, when interpreted in the light of the universal call to holiness, explains most fully the essential characteristics of the Renewal.

For those who open themselves to the Renewal, new life in Christ is related to the spiritual experience called "Baptism in the Holy Spirit," the "Outpouring of the Spirit" or the "Release of the Holy Spirit." The term "Baptism in the Holy Spirit" (cf. Mark 1:8; Acts 1:5; 11:16) needs, of course, more precise description. The term has become in the Charismatic Renewal as a whole—apart from French and Italian speaking areas in which "Outpouring of the Spirit" is more commonly used—the term of description for this primary experience with the Holy Spirit.[1]

2.1.1. A Grace of Pentecost

"Baptism in the Holy Spirit" is a concrete experience of the "Grace of Pentecost," in which the working of the Holy Spirit becomes an experienced reality in the life of the individual and of the faith community.

---

[1] For a clarification of the term "Baptism in the Spirit" (e.g., an initial exegetical/patristic study): *Christian Initiation and Baptism in the Holy Spirit: Evidence from the First Eight Centuries*, Kilian McDonnell and George T. Montague (2nd ed., Collegeville: The Liturgical Press, 1995).

The experience of "Baptism in the Holy Spirit" is the certain and sometimes overwhelming "realization" of the loving nearness of God proclaimed in the Church's message and encountered in the individual act of faith.[2] It is a threshold of spiritual life that is crossed, bringing trust in the Father and a desire to being open to the teaching of the Holy Spirit. It constantly deepens our faith, so confirming our "conviction about things we do not see" (Heb 11:1) and making possible the perception of God's effective presence. This experiential perception reveals God in His immense incomprehensibility as well as in His loving and Fatherly care. This revelation of God attracts, opens new categories of thought, reveals new goals and desires, makes clear the significance of God's Will as well as of human sinfulness and the need for repentance. This experience is similar to that of St. John of the Cross when he states: "I think that one who has not experienced it cannot well understand it. But the soul that experiences it, seeing that what is deeply felt still remains to be understood, calls it 'an indefinable something': since it cannot be understood, it cannot be expressed, but it can very well be felt."[3]

Often accompanied by speaking in tongues ("glossolalia") (cf. 1 Cor 14), this experience is sometimes also accompanied by tears. It is an experience which does not exclude the human emotions discovering God's goodness and mercy. It is a spiritual experience of thirst, which finds its satisfaction in the one, true inner spring, an immense, peacefully flowing river in which to be immersed (cf. John 7:37ff.). These and other empirical effects of the gift of the Holy Spirit can, for many members of the Renewal be specifically dated. They are bound to an event which is experienced as an intervention that is intellectually and emotionally localized. The "Outpouring of the Holy Spirit" is a decisive introduction to a renewed perception and understanding of God's presence and ac-

---

[2] "Experience," as here described, transcends the purely outward or objective dimension of personal salvation history. Grace and the gift of the Holy Spirit need to be "realized," as John Henry Newman expresses it (cf. John Henry Newman, *Grammar of Assent*).

[3] Cf. *Spiritual Canticle* (VII, 10), in which St. John of the Cross is not strictly speaking of the "Outpouring of the Holy Spirit," but of the mystical fellowship with Christ.

tion in personal life and in the world. It is, in short, the experiential rediscovery, *in faith,* that Jesus is Lord by the power of the Spirit to the glory of the Father. Rooted in baptismal grace, "Baptism in the Spirit" is essentially the experience of renewed communion with the divine Persons. It is an opening up, and unfolding of Trinitarian life in the baptized.

With such experience, however, it is not just emotions that are in play. The individual is illuminated with a new light of self-understanding. The experiential transcends the emotional dimension, even when the emotional faculty of the individual can be deeply affected. Such experience has unquestionably its rightful place and meaning for the faith-life of the Christian. It is possible that in this way the objectively valid and given elements of the faith—especially the election and call to grace and its confirmation in the Sacrament of Baptism—become subjectively more obvious and understandable.

The prayer for "Outpouring of the Spirit" is a prayer of personal surrender to Jesus Christ the Lord. It occurs most often in the context of the intercessory prayers of the members of a prayer community. Here the *communio*-dimension of God's Spirit comes to expression. He usually chooses the path of mediation through brothers and sisters in faith, that is, through the faith community of the Church. He does not isolate from the Church in its concrete expression of community, but rather He binds the faithful together into this community. In fraternal communion and with trust in the goodness of the Lord inspired by their own experience, the members of the faith community help the individual to surrender simply and deeply to the action of the Holy Spirit. This prayer is generally accompanied by the gesture of laying hands on the head or shoulder of the person. This expresses communion, fraternal and caring proximity and encouragement. The laying on of hands is not a sacramental rite, although this gesture is often present in the celebration of Sacraments. It is, rather, an everyday gesture that the Judeo-Christian Tradition has always known and practiced.

It must be further added that "Baptism in the Spirit" is a free and unmerited gift of God and is usually the fruit of a free decision, a step of conversion, an act of entrusting everything to Christ the

Lord, of giving one's whole life to Him so that He might transform it. It is also the decision to surrender to the Holy Spirit, without setting any limits on divine free action, a decision to receive in faith the fullness of God's grace. For the faithful, this is simply a way of reviving the grace of Baptism, which is often, as it were, laying dormant within the soul, and allowing it to produce all its potential fruit. "From the moment of our Baptism, grace is hidden in the depths of our intelligence, its presence concealed even from inner perception; but when we begin to desire God with all our strength, then, in an inexpressible word of the mind's inner perception, it lets the soul share in its good things."[4] Too often baptized individuals have not had a genuine living encounter with the Lord; "the initial evangelization has often not taken place," and there is still no "explicit personal attachment to Jesus Christ" (CT 19). "Baptism in the Spirit" therefore, as renewal of baptismal grace in a personal encounter with the Lord Jesus, does not replace the need for catechesis, but demands it. When no such catechesis in the basic elements of the Catholic faith has taken place, it must be supplied. A continuation of this catechesis is, of course, also necessary. The fundamental decision to entrust in faith one's life to Jesus Christ necessitates as well an increasing factual knowledge of His person, His teachings and His saving deeds; in other words, knowledge of His Word and of the teachings of His Church. This generally occurs in the prayer groups and communities of the Renewal through "Life in the Spirit Seminars." This catechesis for adults is often spread over several weeks, its aim being not only to recall the main elements of the faith, but also to inspire a more personal commitment to the Lord Jesus and the expectation of a Pentecostal experience of His Holy Spirit.

It is always a difficult matter to analyze religious experience, especially since it varies greatly from person to person. It is in the fruits of such experience that it becomes evident to what degree religious experience contributes to a true renewal of Christian life. Spiritual tradition teaches that believers often have to endure periods—sometimes even extended periods—of inner dryness

[4] Diadochus of Photicea, *A Hundred Chapters*, LXXVII; SCh 5 bis: 135.

and barrenness, periods which seem to be without significant spiritual experience. This dryness cannot always be interpreted as resulting from a lack of openness to the Holy Spirit. The spiritual masters teach that believers can glorify God by their faithfulness, especially in those times when they seem to be deprived of the comfort of God's presence.

Finally it must be recognized that the deepened "realization" of the personal relationship to Jesus Christ, which is referred to in the Renewal as "Baptism in the Holy Spirit" or "Outpouring of the Holy Spirit," does not belong to any particular movement, but to the Church, which celebrates the Sacraments of Initiation.

2.1.2. Theological Interpretation

"Baptism in the Holy Spirit" is an expression of a reality which has not yet been completely clarified. What follows is an attempt to contribute to future reflections in our effort to understand the reality of "Baptism in the Holy Spirit" in the light of the theology and the living Tradition of the Church. It may sometimes appear to be a novelty of our time, but there is evidence of this experience throughout the history of the Church. There are threshold-moments in the life of believers in all ages of the Church of a living encounter, a real perception, a taste and an enjoyment of God.

1. The Church holds that the Sacraments of Baptism and Confirmation together with the Eucharist are the Sacraments of Initiation into the communion with God and into the fellowship of God's people.[5] Nevertheless theologians make a distinction between the "bath of new birth" (cf. Titus 3:5) and the conferring of the Holy Spirit by the laying on of hands (e.g., Acts 19:1-7) which has been clearly established by biblical and patristic scholarship. These two appear in Christian initiation either together or separate, but related to each other (cf. Acts 10:44-48).

2. In movements within the Church and outside of it "Baptism in the Holy Spirit" is used in a number of senses. Here we

[5] *Catechism of the Catholic Church* (Vatican City: Libreria Editrice Vaticana; Collegeville, The Liturgical Press, 1994) no. 1212.

point to two senses. First, there is a rather broad usage of "Baptism in the Holy Spirit" referring to the experience of receiving the prophetic gifts, usually tongues or prophecy, generally through the laying on of hands in a non-sacramental context. Second, "Baptism in the Holy Spirit" is used referring to the experience of receiving the Holy Spirit with the life of grace, together with the reception of the charisms, as an integral part of Christian initiation or as a later reappropriation, or stirring up, in a non-sacramental context of what was already received at initiation.[6] In this document we understand "Baptism in the Holy Spirit" in this second sense, unless otherwise indicated.[7]

3.   If one is speaking only of a certain subjective experience this is not a sacrament, though it may accompany true sacramental action or the reappropriation of initiation. The subjective experience, therefore, cannot be regarded as by itself necessary for becoming a Christian.

4.   Given the close relation of "Baptism in the Holy Spirit" in the second sense to Christian initiation, it is clear that "Baptism in the Holy Spirit" does not belong to any movement within the Church, but to the Church itself.

5.   While maintaining the close relation of initiation to the reception of the charisms, we must also say that the charisms are never bound in an absolute sense to the Sacraments. Nor are the charisms "things." Charisms are the way the Spirit comes to "visibility" in the service of the Church and the world. For a number of reasons, the charisms may at

---

[6] It is clear that in initiation the reception of the Holy Spirit with the life of grace belongs to a more primary order of religious reality than the reception of the charisms, prophetic or non-prophetic. Therefore one can say that the reception of the Holy Spirit with the life of grace is the primary reality, while the charisms are the secondary realities.

[7] For a clarification of the term "Baptism in the Spirit" see, among others, the exegetical/patristic study by Kilian McDonnell and George T. Montague, *Christian Initiation and Baptism in the Holy Spirit: Evidence from the First Eight Centuries* (2nd ed.; Collegeville: The Liturgical Press, 1995).

one moment be dormant, or not fully operative. The reappropriation of one's Sacramental Baptism may be a graced moment when the charisms manifest themselves as an experienced reality. This experience, which embraces the intellect, will and emotions, is often accompanied by a realization that Jesus is Lord. In most cases this sense of Presence is accompanied by an experience of Power which is spontaneously identified with the power of the Holy Spirit. This Power is sensed as in direct relationship to mission. This is manifested in a bold faith, inspired by love, which makes one capable of undertaking and accomplishing great things for God's Kingdom. Still another characteristic result of this awareness of Presence and Power is the intensifying of a life of prayer, in which one is especially attracted to the prayer of praise. This renewing experience is generally perceived as a kind of resurrection which often expresses itself in joy and enthusiasm. This does not, of course, preclude experiencing the cross (cf. 2 Cor 4:10). And, above all, it must be maintained by an on-going repentance (*metanoia*).[8]

6. This "Outpouring of the Spirit"—rightly understood—will not obscure the fact that the individual, who approaches God, is approaching an objective Person. The one seeking is pointed to a Reality which necessarily transcends his own limitations, a Reality which cannot be "grasped" by the experience, emotions or intellect of the human individual. God has revealed Himself in the Word and in salvation history. "God's eternal power and divinity" (Rom 1:20) have indeed become "visible" and are therefore, for every individual, objective truth; God cannot be reduced to that which is subjectively experienced. Every reality, which a person confronts, transcends his individual intellectual and emotional capacity to comprehend. How much more is one limited when confronted by God's infinite Existence and Personality. Therefore, the fundamental support of "subjective evidence" for the act of faith, as it occurs in the "Baptism of the Holy

---

[8] Léon-Joseph Cardinal Suenens, *Lumen Vitae* (Brussels, 1974) 379.

Spirit," cannot dispense from the necessity of endeavoring to understand and accept the "objective content of faith" which has been revealed.

7.   In water Baptism the individual is born to new life. It is the Sacrament, which accomplishes and testifies to this event of faith, even when this spiritual beginning remains hidden to purely human perception. On the other hand, spiritual reality can become tangible in the empirical dimension. The baptized can grasp in the depths of his heart that God is at work in his life, and his fellow Christians can see this in his behavior. It is possible in this way that the grace of Baptism can be experienced in discernible charisms which "build up the body of Christ" (Eph 4:12).

Ecclesial tradition is aware of diverse expressions which encompass this manifestation of spiritual reality or try to put into words its effect:

—"Wisdom, which instructs, makes wise and leads to perfection"[9] —Origen;
—"Anointing, which enables a knowledge of all spiritual reality"[10] —Didymus the Blind;
—"Wisdom, which reveals Christ in all his greatness"[11] — Basil the Great;
—"Faith, which is not only dogmatic, but which accomplishes deeds that exceeds human capacity"[12] —Clement of Alexandria.

Even if these terms, which are merely indicative and which could easily be multiplied using the writings of the Early Fathers, seem to be abstract, nevertheless they intend to encompass the very concrete change in the life of the faithful, which is accomplished by the reception of new life in Christ.

8.   It is the gift of the Spirit which intervenes in the life of those to be baptized and produces this change of life. His

[9] On First Principles 1.3.8; SC 252, 162.
[10] On 1 John 2:18-19; PG 39, 1784.
[11] On the Holy Spirit 18,46; SC 17 bis. 410.
[12] On John, fragments; PG 74:59

descent upon the individual causes the renewal of the spiritual and intellectual nature. Again theological terms may help to better understand this event. Those terms which are used in the Scriptures have particular strength and reliability in this regard:

—"Anointing with the Holy Spirit" (Isa 61:1; Luke 4:18; Acts 10:38; 2 Cor 1:21ff.; 1 John 20:27);
—"Outpouring of the Holy Spirit" (Isa 32:15; Ezek 39:29; Zech 12:10; Acts 2:16; 10:45; Rom 5:5; Titus 3:5ff.);
—"Baptism in the Holy Spirit" (Isa 1:16; 44:3ff.; Ezek 36:25ff.; Mark 1:8; Acts 1:5; 11:16).

The Tradition of the Church as well shows the importance of this spiritual experience for growth towards perfection. It is shown as a threshold of conversion, a gripping encounter with the Lord Jesus or as the delicate touch of the Holy Spirit, leading the faithful to ever greater teachability.[13]

9. It is lastly the Church which gives the faithful, searching for spiritual experience, irreplaceable guidance and orientation; the individual as well as the group, both fallible in their understanding, finds in the Community of Faith the reliable interpretation of the Word of God and His binding instruction. Alone the Church is able to guarantee the truths of the Faith, for to her is given the promise of the Lord, that He would keep her in the truth (cf. *LG* 12). Therefore the individual and the apostolic community remain dependent upon the Church.[14]

[13] A broad and very illuminating treatment of the fundamental experiences with God as they appear in the Old and New Testaments can be found in *Herrlichkeit. Eine theologische Ästhetik* by Hans Urs von Balthasar (Teil 1, Einsiedeln 1967; Teil 2, Einsiedeln 1969) or the English translation titled *The Glory of the Lord: a theological aesthetics* translated by Erasmo Leiva-Merikakis, ed. by Joseph Fessio and John Riches (New York: Crossroads Publications, 1983).

[14] To understand better the reality of "Baptism in the Holy Spirit," one may look to what in Christian Tradition is often called "a second conversion" (cf. Clement of Alexandria, *Stromate* 7,10; *PG* 9, 477–84). This may occur suddenly, as in the life of St. Francis of Assisi at St. Damiano, as for St. John of God, who was touched by a sermon by Blessed John of Avila; for St. Francis Borgia in front of the corrupt body of Queen Isabella of Spain. It can also be prepared for by spiritual exercises like those proposed by St. Ignatius of Loyola. Cf. article of H. Pinard de la Boullaye, "Conversion," *Dictionnaire de Spiritualité* II/2 (Paris, 1953) 2224–65.

2.2. The Fruits of "Baptism in the Holy Spirit"

2.2.1. The Rediscovery of the Scriptures

One of the prime fruits of "Baptism in the Spirit" is a renewed taste for Holy Scripture. The word always binds the speaker with the hearer. In God's Word, the faithful therefore encounter Jesus Christ in person. Still more, He, who is God's Messenger, is Himself the Incarnate Word of God. Many believers have witnessed to this discovery or rediscovery of the Scriptures as the living Word of God. The texts take on a new clarity and vigor, they become relevant and nourishing for the heart and life of the believer. The "breath of the Holy Spirit" makes the words of Jesus once again experiential as what they in truth are: "spirit and life" (John 6:63), a spring inexhaustibly welling up.

It is normal that, in reviving the grace of Baptism and renewing personal commitment to Jesus Christ, the "Outpouring of the Spirit" should restore this taste for Scripture, this need to be nourished by every Word coming from the mouth of God: "It is true that being a Christian means saying 'yes' to Jesus Christ, but let us remember that this 'yes' has two levels: it consists in surrendering to the Word of God and relying on it, but it also means, at a later stage, endeavoring to know better and better the profound meaning of this word" (CT 20). It is in diligent and persistent contact with the texts themselves that the faithful, guided by the Holy Spirit, receive the bread of the Word of God. This Word is an essential nourishment, always relevant, always given, satisfying all the longings of the soul, strengthening the hearts of believers, enlightening minds and nourishing faith. Scripture is "a pure and lasting fount of spiritual life" (DV 21). It is by meditating on the texts in the light of the Tradition of the Church and with openness to be taught by her Magisterium that we come to real understanding; for recourse to Scripture, as light for all the baptized, cannot be left only to personal interpretation (cf. 2 Pet 1:20) or to a partial and selective reading of its texts. That is why priests and competent lay people in the Renewal must develop and maintain this knowledge of Scripture in the light of the Church's teaching.

The Church has received from her Lord, in and through the Holy Spirit, the mission and the grace to recognize the voice of her Spouse in the texts of the Bible and to faithfully communicate it. All the books of the Old and the New Testaments, in the great diversity of their authors and literary forms, "written under the inspiration of the Holy Spirit, . . . have God as their author" (*DV* 11). Holy Scripture is therefore one. Certain texts cannot be singled out or favored to the detriment of others or read in isolation. The reading of Scripture should be deep and searching, viewing passages in their context and respecting the sense given them by their author and their historical context. For this reason the texts must always be read in the light of the Tradition and Teaching of the Church.

The Renewal has at times been accused of "fundamentalism," that is, of an approach to Scripture that is too literal and too immediate. It is true that members of the Renewal, while having a living faith in the power of God, are not always adequately aware of the created means God employs to mediate that power and do in fact sometimes take a too narrow approach to the Bible. It is especially important that texts of the Bible not be read in isolation or be ascribed a "magical" character. An isolation from other texts, which are related to it, isolation from the living Tradition of the Church, or isolation from well-founded human knowledge which bears on the text, can lead to false understanding. All of this being said, however, it must be insisted that God's Word be taken seriously "not as the word of men, but as it truly is, the word of God . . . ." (1 Thess 2:13). Belief in the historical truth of the Gospels and in the authenticity of miracles (cf. *DV* 19) cannot be simply dismissed as fundamentalistic.[15]

Love and understanding of the Scripture is the heritage of the saints in the Church. Persistent and devoted reading of the Word of God, together with regular participation in the Sacraments is indeed a privileged path to holiness and to the fulfillment of Christ's evangelistic commission. By trusting in the truth of Scripture, the faithful receive new energy to grow in faith, to find enlightenment for the many aspects of their daily life, and to draw from the divine well-spring of charity. The Christian who clearly communicates to

---

[15] Cf. Pastoral Document of the American Bishops (Washington, 1984) no. 33.

fellow believers what God expects in a specific situation, is speaking, according to the New Testament, "prophetically," building up the Church (cf. 1 Cor 14:3), "correcting, reproving, appealing" (2 Tim 4:2); his words will bring comfort, call to repentance and awaken hope.

2.2.2. Renewed Interest in Prayer and the Sacraments

Another evident fruit of "Baptism in the Holy Spirit" is a renewed interest in prayer. Prayer is "at once personal and shared in community praise and intercession, which tries to be both contemplation and a source of evangelization."[16] Prayer is experienced as a well-spring of the spiritual life: prayer coming from the heart, transcending all sterility and merely routine prayer of praise, "the fruit of the lips" (Heb 13:15), springing from love's fascination with the works of God, seeking "to give thanks to God always" for salvation in Christ (1 Cor 1:4); prayer of intercession, trusting and simple; prayer of the community, arising from the need to pray together in the fellowship of faith.

Also to be mentioned, as one of the often and normally experienced effects of the Spirit's work, is prayer in tongues ("glossolalia"). Prayer in tongues is a fruit of confident surrender to the Holy Spirit and brings with it new forms of prayer. St. Paul teaches that there can be "prayer in the spirit" which is not of the mind (1 Cor 14:14). By praying in tongues, the spirit of the one praying is uplifted (cf. 1 Cor 14:4), even if the "mind contributes nothing" (1 Cor 14:14). Experience shows that those who pray regularly in this way are indeed nourished and strengthened in the spiritual life. This prayer in tongues cannot be a substitute for the habitual practice of prayer of the heart, which builds up the interior life of the faithful.

Such prayer, not being on the conceptual level of the intellect, is humble and simple. This is experienced when one no longer knows how to pray. St. Paul states: "The Spirit too helps us in our weakness, for we do not know how to pray as we ought; but the Spirit himself makes intercession for us with groaning that can-

[16] Pope John Paul II, Address to the Bishops from the South of France, December 16, 1983.

not be expressed in speech" (Rom 8:26). Prayer in tongues is one of the ways in which the Holy Spirit aids in overcoming human limitation in prayer.

In this regard it is necessary to distinguish between prayer in tongues, which often develops into singing in tongues, from speaking in tongues, which during the assembly requires "interpretation," so that the Church may be edified or built up (1 Cor 14:5). The "speaking" in this latter case serves to attract attention to the message of the interpretation.

This rediscovery of prayer in all its forms is the reason for the formation and development in the Renewal of countless prayer groups throughout the world. The essential feature of so-called "charismatic" prayer is not primarily spontaneity or improvisation, but the consciousness of the leading and presence of the Holy Spirit. This attitude of prayer in the Holy Spirit includes a disposition of attentiveness. All forms of prayer—from the most liturgical to the most private—find renewal when they are viewed and experienced as a gift from God. Care must be taken, however, not to encourage, under pretext of creativity and spiritual freedom, forms of prayer whose expressions would not be in conformity with the tradition and experience of the Church. Without stifling the Spirit or restraining a legitimate spontaneity, those who have pastoral responsibility must help to ensure that prayer remains authentic. This necessitates that they themselves are men and women of prayer, solidly rooted in the rich and manifold spiritual heritage of the Church.

Another evident fruit of the Spirit's renewed presence in the lives of Catholics has been a rediscovery of the importance of the Sacraments, especially the Sacraments of Reconciliation and the Eucharist. "Through the Church's sacraments, Christ communicates his Holy and sanctifying Spirit to the members of his Body."[17] A deeply spiritual life can grow and persevere more readily in the midst of an increasingly difficult social environment through a renewed sacramental practice. The development of a deepened prayer life brings with it this deepened sense of the efficacy of the Sacraments for spiritual growth.

[17] *Catechism of the Catholic Church*, no. 739.

Thirst for sacramental life goes together with love for the liturgy and its importance for the Christian life and for its ecclesial character. One of the blessings of the Renewal has been this new appreciation for the beauty of the liturgy, of its sacred character and its evangelizing power. At times "charismatic liturgies" have tended to borrow too heavily from popular culture and lack something of the sacredness which is appropriate to the liturgical worship of the living God. The Renewal must be encouraged in developing an ever deeper sense for the liturgical traditions of the Church as well as an understanding for the liturgical renewal of the Second Vatican Council.

2.2.3. *Prayer for Deliverance*

A further dimension of the spiritual life of the renewal in the Holy Spirit is the spiritual combat against the "works of darkness" (cf. Eph 5:11). After His Baptism, Jesus was "driven" by the Spirit (cf. Mark 1:12) into the wilderness, where He was confronted by the Evil One. The Charismatic Renewal is rediscovering what the Church has never ceased to profess: "Our battle is not against human forces but against the principalities and powers, the rulers of this world of darkness, the evil spirits in regions above" (Eph 6:12). We must not deceive ourselves by ignoring the fact that a hard struggle against the powers of darkness runs all through history . . . and will go on to the last day (*GS* 37).

This struggle against evil spirits, whose reality cannot be doubted,[18] has at times been given undue emphasis by some in the Renewal. The experience and the wisdom of the saints teach that it would be naive to ignore the existence and the influence of demons. But neither should their power or importance be overestimated or their presence be suspected in every situation of spiritual crisis. The victory of Christ and the authority He has given His Church provide us with the means to overcome Satan and his dominions: the Sacraments (especially the Sacrament of Reconciliation), the sacramentals, prayer and fasting. Consciously renouncing sin, rejecting the Evil One and all his works are ways

---

[18] This is attested to among other things by the exorcism in the Rite of Baptism.

in which the faithful share in the prophetic mission of Christ and His victory over the Prince of this World. In this combat against the "powers of darkness," an attempt should be made to avoid the spectacular. It is especially important to always give deference to the reserved and mandated authority of official exorcists appointed by the Church (cf. *LG* 35; *CL* 14).[19]

2.2.4. *Love for and Commitment to the Church*

There are numerous reasons that Christians today become particularly sensitive to what seems archaic and cumbersome in ecclesial institutions, as well as to defects among the faithful, both clergy and laity, with whom they come into contact. Parishes and various groupings in the Church sometimes appear to be lacking in spiritual vigor. Pastoral care will aim at helping Catholics to understand and appreciate the richness of their Catholic heritage. They need purification and pruning in order to bear fruit and reach maturity.

The "Outpouring of the Spirit" brings with it a rediscovery of the Church as the living Body of Christ. "It is in the Church that Christ fulfills and reveals his own mystery as the purpose of God's plan: 'to unite all things in him' (Eph 1:10)."[20] A new love for and sense of the Church leads many, who have experienced it, to a renewed desire to give themselves more in service to the Church. The Spirit, who anointed Jesus in His humanity and in His Mystical Body, the Church, draws all the baptized to a closer union with each other, that is, with the whole people of God.

The Second Vatican Council emphasizes this importance of the Church when it states: "At all times and in every race, anyone who fears God and does what is right has been acceptable to him. He has, however, willed to make men holy and save them, not as individuals without any bond or link between them, but rather to make them into a people who might acknowledge him and serve him in holiness. He therefore chose the Israelite race to be his own people and established a covenant with it. He gradually instructed this people . . . . All these things, however, happened as a preparation

---

[19] Cf. Declaration of the Congregation for the Doctrine of the Faith (December 2, 1985) on exorcism.
[20] *Catechism of the Catholic Church*, no. 772.

for and figure of that new and perfect covenant which was to be ratified in Christ, . . . the Covenant in his blood; he called together a race made up of Jews and Gentiles which would be one, not according to the flesh, but in the Spirit" (*LG* 9).[21]

It is therefore important for Catholics in the Renewal to have a clear understanding of what the Church is. The *Catechism of the Catholic Church* states: "In Christian usage, the word 'church' designates the liturgical assembly (cf. 1 Cor 11:18; 14:19, 28, 34, 35), but also the local community (cf. 1 Cor 1:2; 16:1) or the whole universal community of believers (cf. 1 Cor 15:9; Gal 1:13; Phil 3:6). These three meanings are inseparable. 'The Church' is the People that God gathers in the whole world. She exists in local communities and is made real as a liturgical, above all a Eucharistic, assembly. She draws her life from the Word and the Body of Christ and so herself becomes Christ's Body."[22]

This love of the Church witnessed in the Renewal is expressed by encountering the Church's inexhaustible wealth of doctrine, her spiritual and liturgical riches, her unfailing resources for bringing life to all aspects of human existence. "Baptism in the Holy Spirit," therefore, brings a rediscovery of the communion of the saints. The saints in glory become—or become once again—friends, brothers and sisters who are caring and close, who draw us closer to Christ and help us to follow Him more completely along the path to holiness. For many, the words of St. Thérèse of Lisieux: "In the heart of the Church, my mother, I shall be Love," have taken on new meaning.

A new sensitivity of being a member of the Church leads the baptized to serve in charitable, social, cultural, catechetical or missionary endeavors. One of the fruits of the "Outpouring of the Spirit" and of the renewal of baptismal life is a new and at times painful awareness of the material and spiritual needs of our time, a sensitivity to the human plight. The Spirit of Jesus not only gives the desire to respond to these needs, but also stimulates creativity and gives new strength and readiness to meet them.

---

[21] Cf. Acts 10:35; 1 Cor 11:25.
[22] *Catechism of the Catholic Church*, no. 752.

2.2.5. Grace and Commission

The Spirit and the fruits of the Spirit are God's free gift. They can be prayed for, but no one has an innate right or claim to them. On the other hand, they become for those receiving them a commission to service. Whoever tries to keep these gifts for himself in order to selfishly enjoy them or to enhance his own reputation, perverts and destroys them. The talent that is buried testifies against the lazy servant and makes him a "worthless lout" (Matt 25:26-30). God's Spirit fell upon the young Church in Jerusalem under the signs of fire and wind. Individual and corporate complacency are grounds for an examination of conscience. Self-contentedness and self-centeredness should be a warning to every group. They awaken doubt whether their enthusiasm is of God's Spirit, who by His very nature is a commission to apostolate.[23]

2.3. Mary, the "Perfect Model" of "Apostolic Spiritual Life" (AA 4)

The Church professes and honors the Mother of God as her most outstanding and unique member. Through her Jesus Christ took on flesh by the power of the Holy Spirit. God's omnipotence created in her that life which is God Himself (cf. Luke 1:32). The divine Pneuma, which "swept over the waters" in creative power (cf. Gen 1:2), overshadowed as well the Virgin of Nazareth as "the power of the Most High" (Luke 1:35); the cloud, which "settled down upon" the tabernacle in the wilderness (cf. Exod 40:35ff.), settled down upon Mary in like manner. For this reason "the holy offspring to be born" of her is "called Son of God" (Luke 1:35). It is therefore just and right when the Church Fathers referred to the Mother of God as "all holy and free from every stain of sin, as though fashioned by the Holy Spirit and formed as a new creature" (LG 56). She represents for the Church the clearest and most unambiguous example of spiritual and apostolic life.

In Mary are seen the fundamental prerequisites of obedience to God's Word which result in the working of the Holy Spirit and the spreading of God's salvation throughout the world. Just as Mary, who "by an angelic communication" received "the glad tidings that

[23] Cf. Chapter 3 of this text to follow.

27

she should sustain (*portaret*) God, being obedient to his word,"[24] so must every Christian open himself to God's message; and because she was obedient, Christ came into her life in order that man might himself through adoption become God's son. Mary therefore has her own special mission in the pilgrimage toward holiness: "How shall man pass into God, unless God has [first] passed into man? And how shall he (man) escape from the generation subject to death, if not by means of a new generation, given in a wonderful and unexpected manner (but as a sign of salvation) by God—[I mean] that regeneration which flows from the virgin through faith?"[25]

The members of the Church therefore, in their search for holiness, turn their eyes to the Mother of God, "who shines forth to the whole community of the elect as the model of virtues" (*LG* 65). "The Church, therefore, in her apostolic work too, rightly looks to her who gave birth to Christ, who was thus conceived of the Holy Spirit and born of a virgin, in order that through the Church he could be born and increase in the hearts of the faithful. In her life the Virgin has been a model of that motherly love with which all who join in the Church's apostolic mission for the regeneration of mankind should be animated" (*LG* 65).

2.4. Pastoral Reflections

2.4.1. Discernment

Pastoral leaders of the Church are sometimes surprised and astounded by new forms and expressions of spiritual life and, as a result, often feel themselves inadequate to the task of the needed pastoral care they present. These new forms of spirituality cannot simply be placed into the already existing and usual categories. The Decree on the Ministry and Life of Priests (*Presbyterorum ordinis*) of the Second Vatican Council states: "While trying the spirits if they be of God, they must discover with faith, recognize with joy, and foster with diligence the many and varied charismatic gifts of the laity, whether these be of a humble or more exalted

---

[24] Irenaeus of Lyon, *Adversus haereses* 5, 19, 1; SCh 153:248.
[25] *Op. cit.*, 4, 33, 4; SCh 100:810–12.

kind. Among the other gifts of God which are found abundantly among the faithful, special attention ought to be devoted to those graces by which a considerable number of people are attracted to greater heights of the spiritual life" (PO 9). Consistent with this admonition of the Council, Pope John Paul II teaches: The priest cannot render his service to the Renewal unless he adopts a positive attitude based on the desire, shared with every baptized Christian, to grow in the gifts of the Holy Spirit.[26] The graces of the renewal in the Holy Spirit for the spiritual life are indeed valuable; they therefore need to be promoted, protected and purified. The advice of St. Theresa of Avila in this regard is that those who have responsibility for the care of souls must have personal experience in the spiritual life as well as the necessary theological wisdom taken from the Scriptures and from the Teachings of the Church and her great Doctors.[27]

The role of pastors includes discernment as well, identifying and distinguishing the call of the Holy Spirit and the possible deceptions of the Evil One. This encompasses also the discernment of that which belongs to the realm of the human psyche and that which is genuinely inspired by the Lord. In discerning, care must be taken, on the one hand, not to judge too hastily, risking the uprooting of good grain with the weeds (cf. Matt 13:29). On the other hand, those in positions of discernment should not be naive, appealing too quickly to the "good fruits" of what may turn out to be unsound.

Pastoral care consists in guiding, nourishing, protecting and stimulating this renewed life of the faithful. This must be done with gentle and reverent care. Those with pastoral responsibility will prudently draw from the wealth of the Church's spiritual tradition with its rich diversity, communicating this to the faithful. They will adapt their counsel to each situation and each person as the situation demands.

It should be stressed that, since the tree is known by its fruits (cf. Luke 6:43, 45), authentic discernment often requires time to allow

---

[26] Cf. Pope John Paul II, Address to the leaders of the Catholic Charismatic Renewal, May 7, 1981, *Insegnamenti di Giovanni Paolo II*, IV,1 (Vatican City: Libreria Editrice Vaticana, 1981) 1126.

[27] Cf. *Autobiography* of St. Theresa of Avila, chapters 13 and 16.

for growth and maturity. Good discernment of persons, groups or situations in the spiritual realm allows for growth and considers not just the beginnings, but also the total process toward maturity. Spiritual life consists of growth and stages of development which include setbacks, defeats and moments of discouragement. The best and most authentically spiritual intentions are not immediately perfect in every respect; they always bear the mark of human limitation. The ordained pastors should never judge according to "appearances" and "hearsay" (Isa 11:3); the "gift of discernment" is only possible to the eye of faith, which perceives the facts correctly and judges them in the light of God's Word. Pastoral care must, for this reason, be patient and understanding. The process of the purification of these intentions is therefore also a concern of the pastor: "Every branch that . . . bears fruit (the Father) prunes to make it bear even more" (John 15:2). This purification must be regarded as a work of God Himself. The pastor can only help to discern it and accompany the one being pruned on his spiritual journey.

In short, the fundamental criteria for discernment are, on the one hand, their conformity with the truth of the Gospel according to the faith of the Church, and on the other hand, the primacy of charity with its fruits of peace, humility, patience, joy and the spirit of service.

2.4.2. The Paths of Spiritual Life

Everything that has so far been observed as fruit of "Baptism in the Holy Spirit" is nothing less than a profound renewal of spiritual and ecclesial life. It is clear that "spiritual life" is not only an individual and subjective matter, but it includes the whole spectrum of Christian life under the direction of the Holy Spirit. The Apostle does not allow any error about the fact that the gift of the Holy Spirit marks the life of the baptized in a clear and recognizable way: "But the fruit of the Spirit is love, joy, peace, patience, kindness, self-control; . . . ." (Gal 5:22ff.). Therefore, vices and sin on the other side, make evident that a Christian, when he is far from God, loses himself.

A renewed life of baptismal grace often brings with it times of dryness and darkness, of trial and temptation. Pastoral care includes personal encouragement to overcome temptation, to be patient in trials and to persevere in faith. Christ calls to renounce one's self, to take up one's cross and follow the true Master of Life (cf. Matt 16:24ff.). It is from the cross that Jesus "delivered over" His Holy Spirit (John 19:30; cf. John 7:39).[28] In the Renewal many have experienced a deeper sense of the centrality of the cross for the Christian life. The glory of the Resurrection and the Pentecostal Outpouring is prepared and preceded by the cross. Participation in the sufferings of Christ is a part of the spiritual life and apostolic witness of every Christian; and so the faithful should be encouraged and aided in freely offering up their own personal suffering for others, rather than seeing these difficult moments of life as defeating or enslaving. As St. Paul states: "I find my joy in the suffering I endure for you. In my own flesh I fill up what is lacking in the sufferings of Christ for the sake of his body, the church" (Col 1:24). Through the Holy Spirit, the saving power of Redemption is constantly at work in the lives of the faithful and includes every aspect of our human experience. This mystery is always deeply personal and individual and must be approached with great care.

There is also the necessity to struggle against one's own defects and sinful inclinations. The asceticism of the Fathers teaches that the struggle to overcome one's passions brings with it the experience of the presence of the Consoler. Life in the Holy Spirit involves as well this personal asceticism and purification. Many in the Renewal have rediscovered the value of the ancient practice of fasting, of perpetual prayer, of radical poverty and a generous sharing of personal resources with the less fortunate.

Temptation, of course, does not come only from within, from the weakness of our human nature wounded by sin, but also from without, from a world filled with idols calling the children of God away from true obedience to their Father in Heaven. Those in the Renewal with pastoral responsibility will therefore cultivate the

[28] This verse (John 19:30) is one of the fundamental theological elements in the rich spiritual content of the Encyclical *DEV* by Pope John Paul II.

sensitivity the Holy Spirit gives to the faithful, enabling them to discern these temptations: misleading ideologies, false spiritual- ity,[29] esoteric or gnostic practices,[30] delusions of the media, false striving after success and wealth, the injustice and destructive- ness of perverse human nature. The scriptural admonition not to be "conformed" to this age or this world (cf. Rom 12:2; 1 John 2:15; 4:4-6) does not mean an anxious withdrawal into a charismatic ghetto. It refers rather to the assurance of victory in Christ, that does not allow the faithful to be overcome by the evil of this age. This strength is available to all who obey the Holy Spirit of wis- dom and strength. "God's gift was not a spirit of timidity, but the Spirit of power, and love, and self-control" (2 Tim 1:7).

2.4.3. Reflections

There are a number of reflections for pastoral and spiritual care of the faithful that are more specifically applicable for the spirit- uality of the Renewal:

1. The strong experience that some have when experiencing "Baptism in the Spirit" needs careful consideration. Like every experience, even when it is fully authentic, this expe- rience of a new, living and intense relationship to the Living God is limited by its very nature. It is given by God's grace at a particular moment of the spiritual journey as an encouragement, as a threshold to a renewed Christian life. Grace becomes tangible, but it does not en- compass the entirety of grace's treasures nor of the Living God who is its source.

   This fact reveals a number of potential dangers. There could arise the temptation to view a particular experience as normative for all spiritual experience—both one's own and that of others. Or again, there is always the risk of in- terpreting spiritual experience according to categories of a theology that does not account for its authenticity in rela-

---

[29] *Catechism of the Catholic Church*, nos. 2113–17.

[30] Léon-Joseph Cardinal Suenens, *Renewal and the Powers of Darkness* (Malines Document IV), (London, 1984) 101, no. 61.

tion to the whole Christian mystery or the mystery of the life of grace in an individual. Even when the Charismatic Renewal is deeply indebted to the faith experiences of many non-Catholic Christians, a Catholic Christian should attempt to interpret his experience of the "Outpouring of the Spirit" in the light of his own Catholic Tradition rather than that of other churches or ecclesial communities. The history of the Church to our day is replete with examples of men and women who were given deep and varied experiences of God's reality and who, in their writings, testified to these experiences with great responsibility and clarity.[31] The advice of such spiritual leaders provides trustworthy criteria for the "discernment of the spirits" and helpful instruction concerning the phenomena of the Renewal.

2. It is important not to set limits to the inexhaustible freedom of the Spirit nor to reduce it to what can be grasped by the human intellect. Rather, it is necessary to exercise discernment concerning the Spirit through the observation of His working (cf. John 3:8). It belongs, moreover, to the life in the Spirit and to the "Gift of Counsel" (cf. Isa 11:1, 2) that one is borne along by God's power while, at the same time, seeking His wisdom. However, when an authentic life of spiritual intimacy with God develops, there can also develop a temptation to go one's own way without sufficiently understanding that the leading of the Holy Spirit, His gifts of counsel and wisdom, are often expressed through others. This was experienced by none less than St. Paul (cf. Acts 9:3ff.) when, after his Damascus-Road-experience, he was sent to Ananias, who would tell him what he had to do.

3. A spirit of individualism and independence can easily lead progressively to spiritual pride and thus to an obstinate insistence upon one's own ways—ways that could lead into error and spiritual bankruptcy. For this reason it is important, especially for those in positions of leadership in the

---

[31] Cf. art. "extase" in *Dictionnaire de Spiritualité* VI (Paris, 1960) 2072–2171 by M. de Goedt; and art. "mystique," *op. cit.*, X (Paris, 1980) 1889–1984, by A. Solignac.

Renewal, to be encouraged to seek wise and prudent counsel from spiritual directors and those in authority in the Church. There are examples of leaders going errant ways because they followed exclusively their own inspirations, however authentic these might have been, without seeking the needed discernment and correction of others. Again St. Paul is the example: "After fourteen years" he "went up to Jerusalem . . . prompted by a revelation." He wanted to lay out to the leaders "for their scrutiny the gospel" as he "presented it to the Gentiles." His reason was abundantly clear. Although he had much experience in the proclamation of the Gospel and had been the recipient of "revelation," he presented both revelation and experience to the "leaders" of the Church for their discernment: ". . . to make sure the course I was pursuing, or had pursued, was not useless" (Gal 2:2).

4. Spiritual experience can also impact the emotional, psychological and physical dimensions of an individual. The whole of one's being is affected at different levels of depth and expression. This should not be considered abnormal nor should there be an attempt made to establish a norm in this regard. Especially in an age, in which psychology is given particular emphasis, there could be a temptation to interpret spiritual experience and the spiritual life as a whole exclusively in psychological categories. Psychology can be helpful and should not be ignored, but it is not sufficient to explain the total mystery of spiritual life. On the one hand, the human person cannot be reduced to psychology; on the other hand, the inner life has its own (psychological) laws and the grace of God usually respects them and works within their context.

5. Intensive emotional reactions and mystical or ecstatic experience, even when they are expressed on the level of the physical (such as tears or laughter), can have a freeing and healing effect in the soul. They can, however, also degenerate into pure sentimentalism, emotionalism or even psy-

chological aberration. Healthy thinking and proper discernment are helpful and necessary to compensate for this potential weakness. The phenomenon of falling (sometimes
referred to as "resting in the spirit") or similar phenomena,
which would appear to bypass the rational level of understanding, could cause one to underestimate the importance
of the specifically rational and illuminative aspect of the encounter with God.[32]

6. The relationship between God's sovereign work of grace and
its expression in empirical phenomena should not neglect
the aspect of God's sovereign freedom. God's free gift of
grace cannot be forcibly achieved through physical mecha-
nisms. Especially the inducing of unusual and strange physi-
cal/psychological phenomena (such as ecstatic dancing and
singing, hysterical shouting and laughing or falling to the
ground in a faint-like state) could turn the progression of
God's gracious working and the physical/psychological results of this working upside down. A provocation of the possible concomitant natural effects of an experience of God's
working could then be confused with the work of grace itself.
Thus the suspicion could be aroused that the gullible are
being manipulated and misused, that the naive are simply
being deceived in their desire for extravagant and unusual
religious experience. A self-seeking hunger for such religious experience would hinder, in such cases, valid spiritual
growth and could even lead to psychological damage.

Saint Theresa of Avila, the great mystic and teacher of the
Church, strongly resists any technique designed to bring
about "ecstasy." "She points up the dangers inherent in some-
one trying to raise his spirit to supernatural and extraordinary
things before the Lord gives the necessary grace. . . . She
states that contemplatives are on a safe road who do not direct
their spirits to sublime things until the Lord himself directs
them. Indeed she does not hesitate to use irony in order to

[32] "Psychologie et extase" by H. Gratton, *Dictionnaire de Spiritualité* X (Paris, 1980)
2171–82 (esp. 2175).

emphasize her position: Whoever thinks himself able by such tricks to achieve a state of ecstasy, apparently hopes that the toad will be able by his own power to achieve flight. God knows only too well how to show himself—when he will; he does not need these little tricks."[33]

The same warning must be given to those who recommend an empty and trance-like state. They recommend "rejection of every physical image, directing their attention rather to a contemplation of divinity."[34] St. Theresa teaches, on the contrary: "The way of highest contemplation must be the humanity of Christ." This must be the content of contemplative prayer—not only during periods of ecstasy or in a state of ecstasy, but also in perfect contemplation.[35]

7.   No such phenomena can be a substitute for a serious Christian life. More importantly, they could be counterfeited and co-opted by evil spirits in a way that leads people into serious spiritual harm. Such phenomena should never be sought for their own sake or for the sake of the sensational. A self-seeking search for such experiences is contrary to the true mysticism espoused by the great saints and teachers of the Church. Authentic mysticism always has the Lord Himself as the focal point—never one's own experience or personal fulfillment.

In the discernment of phenomena in general, the advice of Cardinal Suenens in his sixth *Malines Document* is relevant: "A phenomenon must be presumed to be natural until the contrary can be proved. The obligation to demonstrate the contrary falls on the person who claims that it is supernatural. Such a prudent approach is not a lack of faith, or a sign of unconscious rationalism, but simply a practical application of the Church's traditional teaching on the relation between nature and grace."[36]

[33] *Ibid.*, 2175.

[34] *Ibid.*, 2175.

[35] *Ibid.*, 2153ff.

[36] Léon-Joseph Cardinal Suenens, *A Controversial Phenomenon, Resting in the Spirit* (Dublin: Veritas, 1987).

8.   A final point to be considered is the relationship to God's
        family represented by Mary, the saints, and the angels. It has
        been the conviction and experience of Christians throughout
        the centuries that these citizens of heaven are active partici-
        pants in salvation history, both that of the individual and of
        the whole world. Especially Mary, as Bride of the Holy Spirit,
        is revered by Catholics as the great symbol of redeemed hu-
        manity. She was the first to receive Jesus the Christ into her
        life, and from that moment on she humbly and quietly
        served Him in His work of redemption. Mary has thus be-
        come the Mother and Model of the Church in her universal
        mission to bring the Good News to every creature. The
        Renewal has at times and in various localities minimized or
        neglected this aspect of Catholic spirituality. The result has
        sometimes been that the rediscovery of this truth has tended
        toward extreme forms of spirituality which emphasize pri-
        vate revelation and marginal or secondary aspects of
        Christian faith and life. Even when special or private "revela-
        tion" is authentic and recognized by the Church, it is to be
        received like other charisms, not as a norm for faith and
        practice, but as encouragement to follow Christ more faith-
        fully on the path of Christian vocation and holiness. This
        danger, however, should not hinder Catholics in the Renewal
        to rediscover this important aspect of their spirituality.

All that has been said makes clear that the spiritual life of the
soul cannot be regulated or adjudged by subjective considerations
alone. The "inner" or "hidden self" of the Christian must "grow
strong" through the working of the Holy Spirit in a myriad of
ways—through the revelation of the mystery of God, through the
imparted gift of faith, through the fellowship of the faithful in the
Church, through the objective celebration of the Sacraments.
"Thus," says St. Paul, "you will be able to grasp fully, with all the
holy ones, the breadth and length and height and depth of Christ's
love, and experience this love which surpasses all knowledge, so
that you may attain to the fullness of God himself" (Eph 3:18ff.).

CHAPTER 3

GIFTED FOR MISSION

3.1. The Call to Evangelize

Both as a personal and as a communal experience of Christ the Lord, the Renewal in the Holy Spirit is a breath of Pentecost. One of the evident fruits of "Baptism in the Holy Spirit" is the desire to evangelize, to announce the Good News of salvation to the whole world. All the manifestations of the Spirit experienced in the Renewal—deepening of faith, growth in charity, communion with the Church, exercise of charisms—have as their aim the growth of the Kingdom of God in people's hearts and in the world. The call to individual holiness is inseparably linked to the call to a new evangelization. Growth in holiness brings with it the irresistible urge to bear a living and dynamic witness to the Good News of salvation. Thus holiness and mission are absolutely correlative. The Spirit of God, in making "saints," creates radiant witnesses to the reality of the Risen Christ, giving new strength and creativity to reach all of human society with the spirit of the Gospel.

Missionary zeal is nourished by the holiness of God's people and in turn is a source of growth in holiness. The Second Vatican Council reminds us that "missionary activity flows immediately from the very nature of the Church . . . and bears witness to its sanctity which it both extends and promotes" (AG 6). Saints, through the fullness of their humanity transformed in Jesus Christ, are living witnesses of the Kingdom "to which we are powerfully attracted" (LG 50). "The Church's holiness is the hidden source and the infallible measure of the works of the apostolate and of the missionary effort" (CL 17). The very aim of the mission of Christ and of the Church is the proclamation of the

Gospel so that all human beings may become "a pleasing sacrifice, consecrated by the Holy Spirit" (Rom 15:16).

Jesus Christ, the Messiah, gave Himself on the cross and sent His Spirit of holiness into the world so that every human being might become a sharer in the divine nature. It is not surprising, therefore, that the fundamental call of the Council for the universal holiness of God's people (cf. CL 16) is at the same time an urgent call to a new emphasis on evangelization. The Apostolic Exhortation *Evangelii nuntiandi* is an expression of this fundamental position of the Council. In response to the wishes of the Fathers of the Synod, called to consider the question of this new evangelization (October 1974), Pope Paul VI wanted to give "a fresh forward impulse, capable of creating, within a Church still more firmly rooted in the undying power and strength of Pentecost, a new period of evangelization" (EN 2).

Finally, this call to holiness and evangelization, as fruit of a new Pentecost in the Church, is to be seen in the context of the rediscovery through the Council of the role of the laity. "The vocation to holiness is intimately connected to mission and to the responsibility entrusted to the lay faithful in the Church and in the world" (CL 17). To evangelize is not only to proclaim the Gospel and to call to faith. Pope Paul VI states: "For the Church, evangelization means bringing the Good News into all strata of humanity, and through its influence transforming humanity from within and making it new: 'Now I am making the whole of creation new' (Rev 21:5)" (EN 18). The Pope is pointing up the crisis in our society which calls for renewed efforts of evangelization when he states: "The split between the Gospel and culture is without a doubt the drama of our time" (EN 20).

The needed openness for evangelization arises out of a personal conversion that is on-going. Such conversion includes growth in faith and an unfolding Christian charity leading to a new and creative sensitivity to the manifold material and spiritual needs of men and women everywhere. This gives rise to the primary witness of the Good News through a life personally renewed by the Gospel (cf. 1 Pet 1:13-16). Pope Paul VI often repeated: "Modern man listens more willingly to witnesses than to teachers, and if he does listen to teachers, it is because they are witnesses" (EN 41). This witness of

life in an often indifferent or hostile world presupposes a deep
and committed spiritual life and a willingness to share in solidar-
ity the pain and travail as well as the joys and aspirations of those
to whom the Gospel message is addressed.

It is equally true that the faithful bear this message of new life
in Jesus Christ "in earthen vessels" (2 Cor 4:7). It is therefore important to keep in mind that "it is not ourselves we preach but
Christ Jesus as Lord" (2 Cor 4:5). The Christian is never a witness
to himself or to his own ideas. That is why, in spite of the faults
and failures of those proclaiming the Good News, they must not
hesitate to give witness to "the unfathomable riches of Christ"
(Eph 3:8). In Baptism and Confirmation the faithful receive the
gifts of the Holy Spirit and therefore have received, in spite of
their weaknesses, the strength to bear powerful witness to Christ.

Clearly all the faithful have a commission to be witnesses to the
Gospel, a fact that does not deny that certain Christians have a
particular charism of evangelization for personal or public witness. This charism enables the one who has received it to find the
simple and poignant words necessary to open hearts to receive
the Good News (cf. *EN* 75). "Side by side with the collective
proclamation of the Gospel, the other form of transmission, the
person-to-person, remains valid and important. The Lord often
used it (for example, with Nicodemus, Zacchaeus, the Samaritan
woman, Simon the Pharisee), and so did the apostles. In the long
run, is there any other way of handing on the Gospel than by
transmitting to another person one's personal experience of
faith?" (*EN* 46).

Genuine evangelization is not a proselytizing, which would in-
volve imposing one's own beliefs on others, robbing them of their
freedom to grow in their own convictions. Anyone who has been
deeply moved by Jesus Christ as the saving Gift of the Father for
all humanity will, of course, seek through argumentation to win
others as well. In doing so, that person will always seek to achieve
agreement of faith in freedom, just as the grace of God appeals to
and respects the freedom of each individual.

True interior conversion is, above all, the work of the Holy Spirit.
"Techniques of evangelization are good, but even the most ad-

vanced ones could not replace the gentle action of the Spirit . . . . The Holy Spirit is the principal agent of evangelization: it is He who impels each individual to proclaim the Gospel, and who in the depths of consciences, causes the word of salvation to be accepted and understood" (*EN* 75). Working together with the Holy Spirit, those witnessing to the Good News will also keep Peter's admonition in mind: "Should anyone ask you the reason for this hope of yours, be ever ready to reply, but speak gently and respectfully. Keep your conscience clear, so that, whenever you are defamed, those who libel your way of life in Christ may be shamed" (1 Pet 3:15-16).

Finally, evangelization, as witness to a personal encounter with Jesus Christ, is only authentic to the degree that it is based on the witness of the Church. No one can commission himself to the service of the Gospel. St. Paul asks: "How can they preach unless they are sent?" (Rom 10:15). There is no true evangelization except in communion with the Church. It is through the Church and in communion with the Church that the Holy Spirit bears witness to Christ. "For where the Church is, there is the Spirit of God; and where the Spirit of God is, there is the Church and every kind of grace."[1] Catholic Christians in the Renewal will discover that their efforts to evangelize will bear deep and lasting fruit to the degree that these efforts are rooted in the Church. When evangelization is understood as not only proclaiming the Gospel message (witness) by word and deed, but as the entire process leading from conversion and personal commitment to Jesus Christ and to initiation into the concrete fellowship of the Church, then this ecclesial dimension becomes evident. The Sacraments (especially the Eucharist) take on central importance. The entire history of the Church with its evangelistic and missionary zeal is replete with examples of saints, witnesses filled with great love and veneration for the Most Holy Sacrament of the Body and Blood of Christ. There is an unbreakable bond between Evangelization and Eucharist. "For in the most blessed Eucharist is contained the whole spiritual good of the Church, namely Christ himself, our Pasch, . . . that flesh which is given life and gives life through the Holy Spirit. . . . For this rea-

---

[1] Irenaeus of Lyon, *Adversus haereses* 3, 24, 1; SCh 211:474.

son the Eucharist appears as the source and the summit of all preaching of the Gospel"(*PO* 5).

3.2. Charisms: Gifts for the Growth of the Church

As fruits of Pentecost, charisms have never been absent from the life of the Church. The twentieth century has seen, through a new and intense "Outpouring of the Holy Spirit," also a new and more intense experience of these charisms among God's people in order to minister more adequately to the needs of our time. The Second Vatican Council recognized the importance and necessity of charisms for the life and growth of the Church (cf. *LG* 4; 12). Pope John Paul II writes in his Encyclical *On the Holy Spirit in the Church and the World*: "Recent years have been seeing a growth in the number of people who, in ever more widespread movements and groups are giving first place to prayer and seeking in prayer a renewal of their spiritual life" (*DEV* 65).

3.2.1. The Nature of Charisms

To characterize and understand charisms, the Apostolic Exhortation *Christifideles laici* identifies them with Saint Paul as a "manifestation of the Holy Spirit given to each one for the common good" (cf. 1 Cor 12:7). "Whether they be exceptional and great or simple and ordinary, the charisms are graces of the Holy Spirit that have, directly or indirectly, a usefulness for the ecclesial community, ordered as they are to the building up of the Church, to the well-being of humanity and to the needs of the world" (*CL* 24). In this same document, Pope John Paul II associates charisms with holiness and the mission of the Church: "They are in fact a singularly rich source of grace for the vitality of the apostolate and for the holiness of the whole Body of Christ" (*CL* 24).

People have sometimes considered charisms to be exceptional graces reserved to great saints. It certainly is true that great saints have often manifested specific charisms in their lives. However the recent teaching of the Church indicates that charisms, ordained as they are for the general good, should belong to the normal Christian experience. Priority must always be given to sanctifying grace and to the "theological virtues" of faith, hope and love, which may not include specific experiences of charisms. Nonetheless, charisms are inseparable from the call to holiness for the whole Body of Christ. Since they are given for the growth of this Body, they are especially linked to the mission of the Church and its call for evangelization. They provide a characteristic support for this evangelization, as the Lord Himself indicates (cf. Mark 16:15-20). The New Testament consistently shows that the proclamation of the Good News is supported by accompanying signs (cf. Mark 16:20; Acts 2:22; 8:13; 14:3; 1 Cor 2:4ff.; 1 Thess 1:5; Heb 2:4). Pope Paul VI exclaimed: "May God grant that the Lord will let fall again a rain of charisms, to make the Church fruitful, beautiful, wonderful, able to impress, to win the astonished attention even of the profane world with its tendency to secularism."[2]

Together with other new spiritual movements in the Church today, the Renewal can be seen as a renewed grace of Pentecost, which has contributed to the rediscovery of the importance and necessity of the charisms in the life of the Church. The term "charismatic" has come to characterize this spiritual development. Charisms, however, should neither be underestimated as something secondary, nor should they be exaggerated as something apart from their role of service. "Charisms are to be accepted with gratitude by the person who receives them and by all members of the Church as well. They are a wonderfully rich grace for the apostolic vitality and for the holiness of the entire Body of Christ, provided they really are genuine gifts of the Holy Spirit and are used in full conformity with authentic prompting of this same Spirit, that is, in keeping with charity, the true measure of all charisms" (cf. 1 Cor 13).[3]

For some, charisms are no more than culturally identifiable expressions of human talents, of psychological gifts or recognizable social functions. Others, on the contrary, are tempted to overestimate their supernatural and miraculous character. The truth lies in neither of these extremes. The Holy Spirit does indeed at times powerfully and directly intervene in sovereign freedom in the history and lives of human beings. The freedom and the natural abilities of

---

[2] Pope Paul VI, October 10, 1974.
[3] *Catechism of the Catholic Church*, no. 800.

those, through whom the Spirit works, are thereby never impeded or negated. "The Spirit himself gives witness with our spirit . . . ." (Rom 8:16). The Spirit never takes possession of a person in such a way as to dispossess that person of any part of his personality. The work of the Holy Spirit in a person or in a group is not to be confused with psychological manipulation or conditioning, and still less with certain manifestations that are present in non-Christian or New Age religions of our day. Much more, the Spirit works with an individual who, in his weakness and limitation, becomes a tool in God's hand for the salvation of the world.

3.2.2. Charisms and the Ordained Ministry

It is important not to confuse freely given charisms and the ordained ministry in the Church. These are not interchangeable, even when they are complementary. This does not, however, place them in conflict with each other. Indeed, the hierarchical ministry is itself considered charismatic: Ignatius of Antioch states that he carried out his ministry of proclamation through the power of the Holy Spirit (*Philadelphia* VII); Polycarp of Smyrna is referred to as the "apostolic and prophetic disciple" (*Martyrium Polycarpi* XVI, 2); it is stated of Meliton of Sardes that he "lived completely in the Holy Spirit" (*Eusebius' History of the Church* V, 24, 2, 5). It was the view of the early Christians, that the hierarchical office was not something which limited or hindered the charismatic life of the Church. The *Catechism of the Catholic Church* states that it is the Magisterium's task "to preserve God's people from deviations and defections and to guarantee them the objective possibility of professing the true faith without error. Thus, the pastoral duty of the Magisterium is aimed at seeing to it that the People of God abides in the truth that liberates. To fulfill this service, Christ endowed the Church's shepherds with the charism of infallibility in matters of faith and morals."[4] The *Catechism* further states: "The supreme degree of participation in the authority of Christ is ensured by the charism of infallibility. This infallibility extends as far as does the deposit of divine Revelation; it also extends to all

---

[4] *Catechism of the Catholic Church*, no. 890.

those elements of doctrine, including morals, without which the saving truths of the faith cannot be preserved, explained, or observed."[5]

The hierarchical ministry, then, is a calling and a gift of the Holy Spirit (cf. 1 Cor 12:27-31; Eph 4:11ff.), but in a different way than those charisms that are distributed by the Holy Spirit "to each as he wills" (1 Cor 12:11). The ability to exercise a charism regularly in the service of the assembly is the free and sovereign work of God's Spirit. Such charisms could be given frequently or only periodically, depending upon the particular and momentary needs of the faithful. The "charism" of the hierarchical ministry, on the other hand, is a permanent enabling of the Spirit in the Church for the on-going pastoral care of God's people. God blesses the Renewal with increasing vocations to the priesthood and to religious life. In this way the Charismatic Renewal becomes a personal and a corporate school in which the renewing power of the Spirit becomes effective in calling to and preparation for these vocations. Therefore, the leading of young men and women to vocations is a priority of its apostolic work. In this the Charismatic Renewal in the Catholic Church holds firmly to the conviction that the Lord gave His Church a sacramental structure and the vocations of religious life.

It must be stressed that both the hierarchical ministry and the exercise of the various charisms are necessary components for the growth in holiness and the apostolic witness of God's people. They are distinct but also complementary ministries arising from the Holy Spirit's call and anointing. Charisms bring to the ministry of the Church the unfolding of a sometimes hidden grace, latent within God's people, which can touch hearts, heal souls and bodies, and enlighten minds, so that the preaching of the Gospel proves to be "not a mere matter of words . . . but one of power, . . . carried on in the Holy Spirit and out of complete conviction" (1 Thess 1:5). The hierarchical ministry adds to this spiritual process the needed discernment and pastoral guidance.

---

[5] *Catechism of the Catholic Church*, no. 2035.

3.2.3. The Diversity of Charisms

Charisms are varied and must be viewed in their multiplicity of expression. A given charism never exists in isolation. It is given within the context of service and growth of the ecclesial body in charity and unity. In the Apostolic Exhortation *Christifideles laici*, Pope John Paul II states: "Charisms . . . can take a great variety of forms, both as a manifestation of the absolute freedom of the Spirit who abundantly supplies them, and as a response to the varied needs of the Church in history. The description and the classification given to these gifts in the New Testament are an indication of their rich variety" (*CL* 24) (cf. 1 Cor 12:7-11, 28, 31; Rom 12:6-8; 1 Pet 4:10ff.).[6] They complement each other as well as complementing the various ministries and vocations the Holy Spirit gives to the Church, "unifying her in communion and in the works of ministry" (*LG* 4).

It can occur that the appearance of certain charisms, although given by God, causes concern and uncertainty among some members of the Church who understandably base their faith on more accustomed forms of ecclesial life. The new forms could appear to threaten the faith itself. Nevertheless it has been shown—not least in the light of Church history—that variety in the exercise of faith brings enrichment to the Church, growth in vitality, a rejoicing in God's goodness and renewed missionary zeal. There develops a new depth in the understanding of Truth and a growth in the spirit of Christian Charity, the Truth and Love which are the very foundation of unity in the Church. In short, the charisms, in their rich variety, are given "for the renewal and the building up of the Church" (*LG* 12). Through them, Christ adorns His Church, making her beautiful, presenting "to himself a glorious church, holy and immaculate, without stain or wrinkle or anything of that sort" (Eph 5:27), preparing her for the Marriage of the Lamb (cf. Rev 19:7-9).

---

[6] This plurality of the charisms is seen, for instance, in the fact that St. Paul speaks in the plural of "gifts of healing" or of "various kinds of tongues" (cf. 1 Cor 12:9, 10).

3.2.4. *The Discernment of Charisms*

Charisms need to be discerned. "No charism is exempt from being referred and submitted to the Church's shepherds. 'Their office [is] not indeed to extinguish the Spirit, but to test all things and hold fast to what is good' (1 Thess 5:12, 19-21), so that all the diverse and complementary charisms work together 'for the common good.'"[7] The exercise of the charisms and their fruits must, above all, be in harmony with the Truth of the Gospel and the Divine Charity of Christian service. To be authentic, charisms must demonstrate their agreement with the rule of faith, with Scripture and the Tradition of the Church, with her doctrine and spiritual experience.

The Holy Spirit is closely related to the humanity of God's Son, to His Incarnation. "This is how you can recognize God's Spirit: every spirit that acknowledges Jesus Christ come in the flesh belongs to God" (1 John 4:2). Through Jesus Christ the Spirit is poured out upon the Body of Christ, the Church. The criterion of truth according to this mystery of the Incarnation is that of conformity with the organic nature of the Church's sacramental and ministerial life. "Guiding the Church in the way of all truth and unifying her in communion and in the works of ministry, he [e.g., the Holy Spirit] bestows upon her varied hierarchic and charismatic gifts, and in this way directs her; and he adorns her with his fruits" (*LG* 4).

The truth of the Incarnation also brings with it a sense of rightness and good judgment. These are fundamental for the exercise of the charisms and for their discernment, especially when there is a question of extraordinary gifts. The Holy Spirit, working in absolute freedom and sovereignty, can accomplish signs and wonders. He does nothing that is bizarre, eccentric or, indeed, immoral. "God is a God, not of confusion (tumult), but of peace" (cf. 1 Cor 14:33). Tumult, theatrics and the esoteric are not authentic signs of the Spirit, who is gentle and kind, even when acting with power. St. Paul's admonition, when referring to the use of charisms and the rule of order in the assembly of the faithful, is clear: "Make sure that everything is done properly (decently) and in order" (1 Cor 14:40).

---

[7] *Catechism of the Catholic Church*, no. 801.

Charisms, as gifts of the Spirit of Love, are also recognized by the Divine Love out of which they spring and by the love in which they are exercised. The Holy Spirit, "as love, is the eternal uncreated gift. *In him is the source and the beginning* of every giving of gifts to creatures" (*DEV* 34). Charisms are, as it were, the Breath of God: "You hear the sound it makes but you do not know where it comes from, or where it goes" (John 3:8). That the authentic Breath of God is at work here can be discerned by the loving service a charism renders for the building up of God's people.

As communion with the very life of God, charity is not a charism but the source of charisms. Love is "the way which surpasses all the others" (1 Cor 12:31). The Church has always taught this difference: sanctifying grace (*gratium faciens*) and the charisms (*gratiae gratis datae*) are seen in differentiation. St. Paul shows this in his First Letter to the Corinthians in that he places the treatment of love, the hymn to charity (1 Cor 13), between two treatments of the charisms and their proper exercise (1 Cor 12 and 14). Love and the charisms do not stand opposed to one another. This relationship he states as: "You must want love more than anything else; but still hope for the spiritual gifts as well . . . ." (1 Cor 14:1).

Ordained to the general good and to the growth of Christian communion in charity, charisms are discerned by the fruit of charity they produce. A genuine charism, whether unobtrusive or of a more exceptional nature, touches hearts and opens them to the love of God. Thus charisms are not to be sought for themselves, but for the good of the Church and of those whom the Church is called to serve. They never cause confusion, anxiety or division when they are "exercised in full conformity with the authentic prompting of the Spirit" (*CL* 24).

Extraordinary charisms rarely appear in the form of judgment or condemnation of persons or groups. They may, however, include vigorous calls to repentance or exhortations in cases of wrongdoing. But they always respect personal freedom and privacy and are open to compassion. As manifestations of the Holy Spirit in the service of others (cf. 1 Pet 4:10), charisms always bear their fruit of "love, joy, peace, patient endurance, kindness, generosity, faith, mildness and chastity" (Gal 5:22, 23), even when, because of human weakness and fallibility, they are not always free from the influence of evident human imperfection.

The Apostle Paul admonishes: "Test everything; retain what is good" (1 Thess 5:21). He does not demand absolute perfection from those exercising charisms. Those who have received the gift of charisms usually exercise them in a less than perfect fashion. The charisms and their accompanying mandate for service are opportunities for growth in self-renunciation and humble submission to the Holy Spirit and the leadership of the Church. In the discernment and fraternal correction that are called for, care must be taken to act with patience, kindness and prudence. Here too no attempt should be made to pull up "the weeds" too quickly lest "the wheat" be destroyed in the process (cf. Matt 13:29, 30).

To summarize, openness to experience is one thing, the pursuit of religious experience is quite another. Charisms are a special call to holiness for the faithful, insofar as they are received with hearts open to conversion and the desire for Christian perfection. In turn they are instruments of evangelization, opening hearts to the call of the Gospel. Charisms are not substitutes for "the more excellent way" of charity. But, since they arise out of God's gift of love, they are an expression of the holiness of the Church in her mission in the world.

3.2.5. The Charism of Prophecy

The Charismatic Renewal has in our time pointed to the fullness of the gifts of the Spirit as they were present in the early Church. Together with numerous studies on the development of the Sacrament of Holy Orders, the New Testament foundation and historical unfolding of the various apostolic activities in the Church also came into focus. The Charismatic Renewal in the Catholic Church never doubted the biblical legitimacy of the sacramental structure of the Church. At the same time it realized that the Church would be weakened if its "institutionalism" resulted in imposing "Saul's armor" (cf. 1 Sam 17:38-39) on those exercising ministry. The Renewal has also tried to resist the unavoidable waste of apostolic energy caused by a struggle for power and prestige, a problem that can only be corrected by placing emphasis on faith growth.

The Charismatic Renewal finds its experience confirmed by the texts of Vatican II which state unequivocally that the Holy Spirit distributes "His gifts" (e.g., "special gifts") to each individual. The Council makes reference in this regard to the experience of the early Church in which the charisms or gifts of grace and their appropriate ministries were exercised in the manner reported in the Acts of the Apostles and the letters of Saint Paul.

There was a special place given in the early Church to the charism of prophecy. In the list of ministries, prophets are always mentioned in second place, directly after the Apostles. The question is: What is the ministry of prophets? The term "prophet" is by no means unequivocal. It can be seen in an Old Testament sense, a New Testament sense, and in a sociological sense. Exegetes and systematic theologians point out that two different concepts of the ministry of prophets are to be found in the early Church. Without the necessary reflection, the use of this term in our day could lead to misunderstanding. Because of the ambiguity of this term it is necessary to describe the ministry of the prophet more precisely.

According to Paul, the Church is "built upon the foundation of the apostles and prophets" (Eph 2:20). This was never meant to signify that there were two churches or two structures of authority, or that the prophetic element was the purer Church and was necessarily at odds with the more institutional Church. One cannot oppose the freedom of the Spirit and the canonical order as though they were contradictory or mutually exclusive. The charismatic/prophetic Church is the institutional Church, and the institutional Church is the charismatic/prophetic Church. The biblical texts indicate the presence of signs, wonders and powerful deeds (cf. Rom 15:18ff.; Acts 2:43; Heb 2:4). Without suggesting that the spectacular confirmations of faith were only for the foundational apostolic period, and not for the continuing life of the Church, the texts do differentiate between the earliest years of the Church, and the later period, in which the normality of everyday faith is the focal point.

The gift of prophecy, which is established in the New Testament, remains as a ministry in the Church for "up-building," "encouragement," and "consolation" (1 Cor 14:1-5). In this sense Saint Paul, who never referred to himself as a Prophet but always as an Apostle, and Silas can be viewed as prophets (cf. Acts 15:30-35). Women as well can be seen as exercising this ministry. Prophecy in this sense "'calls to account' the egoistically darkened soul and leads to a new 'understanding,' laying bare 'the secret of the heart,' and leading even to adoration and a realization of God's presence in the Church" (1 Cor 14:24ff.).[8] At least in this "everyday form," the gift of prophecy retains its validity in the life of the Church. It has a profound meaning for proclamation and for awakening a sense of God's working and authority in His people.

The New Testament does not allow, however, for a disjuncture of this ministry from the Church, for an excuse to ply an independent course toward new shores. The gift of prophecy is not self-justifying, but must submit itself to examination (cf. 1 Cor 12:10; 14:29; 1 Thess 5:21; esp. 1 John 4:1). God's Spirit will become self-evident when other spirit-endowed individuals recognize and confirm the faith-intuition of the one claiming to speak prophetically (cf. 1 Cor 14:37ff.). Both the orthodoxy of the prophetic utterance (cf. 1 John 4:2ff.; 1 Cor 12:3) and the living example of the prophet (cf. Matt 7:15-19) are further criteria for discernment. Finally, the effect of the prophecy itself is important. The effect should not be to awaken emotions regarding supposed future events or to illicit religious dread. Rather it should lead to the adoration of the living God: "But if an unbeliever or an uninitiated enters while all are uttering prophecy, he will be taken to task by all and called to account by all, and the secret of his heart will be laid bare. Falling prostrate, he will worship God, crying out, 'God is truly among you'" (1 Cor 14:24ff.).

Consistent with these texts from the New Testament, Vatican II requires the discernment of prophecy, which can only be considered authentic when it has stood the test. It gives "those who have charge

---

[8] H. Schürmann, *"Die geistlichen Gnadengaben,"* in G. Baraúna (ed.) *De Ecclesia. Beiträge zur Konstitution "Über die Kirche" des Zweiten Vatikanischen Konzils* (Bd. I, Freiburg u.a., 1966) 494–519, 507ff.; cf. A.-M. de Monléon, *Charismes et ministères* (Paris, 1995) 101–112.

over the Church" the responsibility to "judge the genuineness and proper use" of the "extraordinary gifts" and their fruits. At the same time, it requires the shepherds of the Church to view the fruit of those charisms, that are truly from God, dispassionately. Still more, the Council obliges the shepherds to receive the manifestations of the Spirit "with thanksgiving and consolation since they are fitting and useful for the needs of the Church" (LG 12).

In our day Pope John Paul II has again reminded the responsible leaders of the Church that God's holy people participate in the prophetic office of Christ. He sees the fulfillment of the prophetic mission of the Church, which is rooted in the Lord of the Church, as a commission of all its members to proclaim the Gospel. This proclamation "takes on various forms in the Church, commensurate with the various charisms each has been given" (cf. Eph 4:11-13). In doing so the Pope calls attention to the fact that "the prophetic mission" retains its validity for the Church in our day and that, "when seen in its fullness, is distributed to men and women alike."[9]

3.2.6. The Charisms of Healing

Among the various charisms there is one group that, in addition to the general rules of discernment, calls for special pastoral attention. The more remarkable charisms can, indeed, become a powerful instrument for evangelization, a special call to conversion and holiness. To this group belong the charisms of healing.

It is clear from the Gospels that the healing of the sick was an integral and important part of the ministry of Jesus. Indeed, it was one of the signs of his messianic mission (cf. Matt 8:16-17; 11:4-6). Jesus, in turn, sent His disciples out as an extension and continuation of His own ministry. They were to proclaim the Good News of the Kingdom and to heal the sick, just as He did (cf. Luke 9:1-6).

Throughout the history of the Church, healing has remained a sign of the Lord's compassion for the sick and suffering (Mark 1:34). These healings were often seen as powerful witness to the personal holiness of those through whose prayer they occurred.

[9] Letter of Pope John Paul II to Priests, Easter 1995, no. 6.

Therefore such miraculous cures were often viewed as special signs of the holiness of certain persons or places. With the arrival of the Enlightenment and of the natural sciences that attempted to view everything from a purely rationalistic vantage, all reports of the miraculous appeared suspect. Their factual accuracy was contested. Even today many people deny the possibility of miracles in general.

In our day, with a view to the multitudes of suffering humanity, the Holy Spirit once again seems to be emphasizing the gifts of healing. These gifts have become an integral part of the experience of the Renewal. The charisms of healing are exercised as a sign of the Holy Spirit's powerful presence in the world and of God's saving will for all. This healing addresses the full complement of human suffering: the spiritual, the emotional, the psychological, and the social—as well as the physical.

Healing is never to be seen as an isolated act. It is a part of the encounter with the living Lord and of conversion of the heart.[10] It is a call to a consistently Christian life, lived in a mutually caring community of faith which is open to receive the riches of God's gifts. The healing of the sick is given as a sign of the presence of the Kingdom and must always be viewed as an integral part of evangelization. Gifts of healing show the compassion of God and open hearts to the saving presence of the Lord. The one who is healed becomes a sign of the working of the Spirit of God (cf. Acts 3:1-10; 4:8-10) and of His healing power.

An understandable human desire for healing could lead, however, to a self-centered attempt to make God an instrument for the fulfilling of personal hopes and aspirations. Healing is never a purely private matter, but is an expression of the power of God present in the Christian community of faith. Therefore, the pastoral care of the community must be extended to the suffering, helping them to seek healing in the context of God's will,[11] which may include selfless suffering as an expression of the cross Christ has invited His followers to take up. "Even the most intense prayers do not always obtain the healing of all illnesses. Thus St. Paul must learn from the Lord that 'my grace is sufficient for you, for my

---

[10] Cf. *Catechism of the Catholic Church*, no. 1504.
[11] Cf. *Catechism of the Catholic Church*, no. 1509.

power is made perfect in weakness . . . .'"[12] The strengthening of the inner spiritual life thus transforms physical suffering, making it into a communion with the suffering of Christ.

The exercise of the charisms of healing, especially when cures are extraordinary, should try to avoid all excesses of sensationalism or emotionalism. These should rather be occasions for grateful praise and humble thanksgiving. Healing should never be sought imprudently or presumptuously, but rather as an enabling gift for renewed service in the Church. Through the gifts of the Spirit, God prepares His people and makes them ready to undertake various tasks and offices for the renewal and building up of the Church. As St. Paul states: "The manifestation of the Spirit is given for the common good" (1 Cor 12:7).

The charisms of healing are as well a free gift of a merciful and gracious God. They are not the result of particular methods or techniques. When, at times, cures are more frequently granted in answer to the prayers of particular persons, such prayers or the persons offering them should not be seen as factors upon which a cure is dependent. And certainly prayers for healing should never stand in opposition to prudent medical advice and treatment by competent physicians.

Healing is part of a holistic spirituality. It always occurs in the context of the more usual elements of the Christian life such as prayer, self-denial and forgiveness. The Sacraments play here a special role, not only the Sacrament of the Sick, whose power to heal is being rediscovered, but also the Sacrament of Reconciliation, which brings inner healing. Both of these Sacraments address the illnesses of body and soul, which are—as modern medicine and psychology have discovered—closely related. Of course, the Eucharist itself is a Sacrament of healing since the Lord of Life is present with His suffering humanity and the power of His Resurrection. "It was our infirmities he bore, our sufferings he endured" (Matt 8:17; cf. Isa 53:4). In His Resurrection His sovereign divinity frees us from the powers of death.

When the Sacraments are given their full and proper place in the life of faith, the charisms of healing will find their rightful

[12] Cf. *Catechism of the Catholic Church*, no. 1508.

54

place in the life of the Christian community. They will be received as a very normal continuation of the ministry of the Lord, which He has entrusted to His Church. When it is recognized through the experience of faith that God can and does heal, the Sacraments themselves will be seen in their full dimension as sources of healing and salvation for all and as living instruments for evangelization.

3.2.7. Charisms and the World to Come

Charisms are given as a witness to the reality of Jesus Christ and for the growth of His Church as the faithful await His coming in glory. This eschatological dimension of St. Paul expresses in his First Letter to the Corinthians: "I continually thank my God for you because of the favor he has bestowed on you in Christ Jesus, in whom you have been richly endowed with every gift of speech and knowledge. Likewise, the witness I bore to Christ has been so confirmed among you that you lack no spiritual gift (*charisma*) as you wait for the revelation of our Lord Jesus Christ" (1 Cor 1:4-7). Only then will the other charisms cease, leaving "love" which "never fails" (1 Cor 13:8).

The renewal of the practice of charisms among the faithful today is an important part of the Church's waiting for "our blessed hope, the appearing of the glory of the great God and of our Savior Christ Jesus" (Titus 2:13). One of the fruits of the Renewal has been a renewed awareness of and desire for the Lord's Coming. This dynamic expectancy gives a future orientation to the Christian life and an urgency to the call to evangelize. "Evangelization cannot but include the prophetic proclamation of a hereafter, man's profound and definitive calling, in both continuity and discontinuity with the present situation" (*EN* 28). Serving all of humanity through evangelization and works of mercy, the members of the Renewal must constantly keep in their hearts this living and blessed hope of the world to come. Man's "true destiny is not restricted to his temporal aspect" (*EN* 28). He is created for eternal communion with the only Absolute Truth that can fulfill his hopes and desires, the Absolute Majesty of the Triune God in an eternity of happiness. Contemporary man, in his lack of orientation and despair, needs more than ever to know that his destiny is not limited to the horizons of this world.

3.3. Forms of Community Life

The grace of Pentecost is a grace of prayer and praise that radiates the proclamation of the Good News (cf. Acts 2:1-42). One of the characteristic fruits of the Renewal in the Holy Spirit has been and remains the forming of prayer groups and communities.

3.3.1. Prayer Groups

Prayer groups, that vary in size and in form of expression, "have multiplied in a surprising way in almost all the dioceses of the world and are one of the greatest riches of the Renewal in the Spirit."[13] They have developed throughout the whole world in the most diverse places and circumstances as living cells of the Church. The diversity of these groups and their members, representing every possible culture and social status, is a sign of their "catholicity." Such prayer groups should be encouraged, recognizing the faithfulness with which many of them have been regularly meeting for years. They are a source of Christian edification, a stimulus for faith and prayer; they offer mutual support and are a form of apostolic witness. The members of these groups are often active in their parishes and in other Catholic organizations. Prayer groups have produced many vocations to the priesthood and religious life. This, too, is a sign that the Holy Spirit is at work through such groups for the good of the whole Church. Priests and bishops should, for this reason, be involved in an active and appropriate pastoral care of these groups.

In situations where such groups are seen to be losing their vitality, this pastoral responsibility becomes evident. Those which are in danger of becoming self-satisfied or self-centered need pastoral help to once again attain the inner dynamic and apostolic fervor of the Christian life. The path to growth and a continued dynamic spiritual life in prayer groups includes an openness for the graces of an ongoing outpouring of the Spirit's power, praise and worship, the exercise of the charisms, active evangelization, an open and heart-felt welcome for new members, and a spirit of humble service among the members themselves.

[13] Declaration of 109 Bishops of Latin America (La Ceja, Colombia, September 4, 1987) no. 62.

Key to the health and spiritual vitality of a prayer group is also, of course, its leadership. Leading a group with its diversity of individuals and activities calls for personal and spiritual maturity, common sense, and Spirit-led discernment. It demands much self-sacrifice and a willingness to serve. Such leadership in a Christian context does not presuppose power or authoritarianism. There should be no room given for rivalry or dissension, especially between leaders of different groups. In this context leadership is understood as servanthood exercised in love. The best guarantee for balance and maturity in the leadership of the Renewal is an adequate theological and spiritual formation, as well as maintained links with other prayer groups and the leadership of the Church and its recognized pastors.

Every baptized individual and every group of the baptized in the Church has the freedom and responsibility to take initiatives and engage in activities that are consistent with and enjoined by the teaching of the Gospel. At times, however, the Renewal has been regarded by some in the Church as a marginal or questionable form of spirituality, and this in spite of repeated positive evaluations by popes and bishops throughout the world for well over twenty years. This should not be cause for prayer groups to become discouraged. Rather it should be an incentive for groups to live consistently and clearly their spirituality, giving testimony to the reality of the Spirit's working in their midst. Neither should it be cause for prayer groups to seek an independence from the legitimate authority of the Church. Following the example and admonition of Pope John Paul II, priests are encouraged to exercise pastoral responsibility for prayer groups: "The priest has a unique and indispensable role to play in and for the Charismatic Renewal as well as for the whole Christian community. His mission is not in opposition to or parallel to the legitimate role of the laity."[14]

It must be clear that prayer groups and their leaders will find the wisdom and direction necessary to fulfill their mission in the world by maintaining close communion with the Church and her desig-

[14] Pope John Paul II, Address to Leaders of the Catholic Charismatic Renewal, May 7, 1981, *Insegnamenti di Giovanni Paolo II*, IV, 1 (Vatican City: Libreria Editrice Vaticana, 1981) 1125.

nated pastors. For this very purpose, the Apostolic See (September 14, 1993) established, as a world-wide service for the Renewal, the International Catholic Charismatic Renewal Services (ICCRS). This is not only a recognition of the calling of the Charismatic Renewal in the Church, it also provides a juridical tool (according to Canon 116 of the *Codex Iuris Canonici*) for the promotion of the Renewal's mission.[15]

3.3.2. Communities

With the renewal of the grace of Baptism and the call to holiness, the experience of the outpouring of the Spirit's power draws some of the baptized to an even more radical commitment in the Christian life. The call to discipleship, which the Gospel enjoins on all, takes the form of a call to community life in the desire for a deeper sharing of prayer, for communion in charity, for a deepening of faith and of witness to the world. In this way, the Renewal has seen and still sees the emergence of communities whose members commit themselves to a way of life that makes them more readily available for the service of the Church.

These communities have various structures, vocations, forms and degrees of commitment and styles of life. This rich variety reflects that of the Church, which, in turn, contributes the balance of its age-old experience and wisdom to the new and emerging communities of our time. In some communities the members intend to live their fellowship to Christ and their link with the Church in a covenant. This means a formal commitment to enter into relationship with other members and to participate in their life-style and mission. The many examples of such new communities strongly reflects the fruit of the renewal in the Holy Spirit, a renewal envisioned by the Second Vatican Council.

Communities are sometimes endangered by a number of factors which are not uncommon to new foundations. The zeal and inexperience of its members often does not contribute to an initial stability in community life. This lack of experience makes it

[15] International Catholic Charismatic Renewal Services (ICCRS) is a private association of the faithful under Pontifical privilege.

equally difficult for founders of such communities to exercise adequate pastoral care. In some cases, a false or naive concept of ecumenism, which is not uncommon in some charismatic circles, envisions a communion in the Holy Spirit that transcends the given limits of a realistic view of the Church and her teachings. There cannot be full communion in the Spirit without communion in the ecclesial Body of Christ which is characterized by a sacramental and institutional structure. For this reason, Catholics hold that the only Church of Christ "subsists in the Catholic Church as something she can never lose" (*UR* 4).

The ultimate aim of all Catholic communities is a life in the fullness of charity and the promotion of the holiness of its members (cf. Rom 12:1; 1 Cor 12:31). Communities have as well the aim to live and witness to their own particular charism in the Church. This implies human and spiritual growth, growth in knowledge and in sound conscience and this, in turn, necessitates conformity to the faith of the Church, communion with the Pope and the bishops, an active sacramental life, and collaboration with other ecclesial groups and communities in the mission of the Church.

For the development of these communities and lay associations five fundamental criteria have been laid down by the Papal Encyclical *Christifideles laici* (*CL* 30):

1. The call to holiness includes "growth towards the fullness of Christian life and the perfection of charity," fostered by "a more intimate unity between the everyday life of its members and their faith."

2. The commitment to profess and promote the Catholic faith in accordance with the Teaching of the Church.

3. "The witness of a strong and authentic communion" with the Pope and the bishops, coupled with a readiness to collaborate with them in pastoral initiatives.

4. "Conformity to and participation in the Church's apostolic goals" to be ever more active as instruments for the evangelization of the world.

5. "Commitment to a presence in human society" as set out in the reflections of the Apostolic Exhortation.

Many of these new communities within the Renewal are already giving strong witness to the concrete fruits that are mentioned in *Christifideles laici*. These fruits are largely the concrete results of "Baptism in the Holy Spirit." In addition to a renewed life of prayer, of sacramental practice and liturgical worship, and of readiness for Christian service in communion with the universal Church, an authentic sign of the Christian vitality of these communities is the renewal of vocations to Christian marriage, to the priesthood, and to consecrated life. Community life must continue to teach and foster the dignity of life as well as the ideals of Christian marriage and the relationship between men and women as they are represented in the texts of the Second Vatican Council (cf. *GS* 47–52).

In cases, however, in which such covenant communities develop in questionable ways, local ordinaries sometimes need to intervene lovingly but firmly in order to correct their course. It is the pastoral responsibility of bishops to oversee the development of these communities who, for their part, need to be open to discernment, correction, and guidance by their bishops.

As a concrete contribution to the need for the close contact of covenant communities with the universal Church, a group of such communities applied at the end of the 1980s for canonical recognition by the Holy See. They were motivated by the desire both to assure greater dialogue and collaboration with each other and to deepen their communion with the Successor of St. Peter, seen as an essential element of their Catholic identity. The result of this application was the establishment on November 11, 1990, of the Catholic Fraternity of Charismatic Covenant Communities and Fellowships as a private association of the Christian faithful under Pontifical privilege.

3.4. Ecumenism and Renewal

The entire history and experience of the Charismatic Renewal in the Catholic Church indicates that the renewal in the Spirit has a special ecumenical calling. The same Spirit of Pentecost who calls to evangelization, inspires Christianity to foster the unity of all Christians and to advance the peace and justice of humanity.

The division among Christians "openly contradicts the will of Christ, scandalizes the world and damages . . . the preaching of the Gospel to every creature" (*UR* 1). The urgency of the call to evangelize points up the urgency and call to reestablish unity among all of God's people.

The Holy Spirit inspires the longing for Christian unity by first awakening in the faithful a sense of the need for conversion of heart. "There can be no ecumenism worthy of the name without interior conversion. For it is from newness of attitudes of mind, from self-denial and unstinted love, that desires of unity take their rise and develop in a mature way . . . . The faithful should remember that they promote union among Christians better, that indeed they live it better, when they try to live holier lives according to the Gospel. For the closer their union with the Father, the Word and the Spirit the more deeply and easily will they be able to grow in mutual brotherly love" (*UR* 7).

The foundation of unity among Christians is to be seen in the Sacrament of Baptism: "By the sacrament of baptism a person is truly incorporated into Christ and into his Church and is reborn to a sharing of the divine life. Baptism, therefore, constitutes the sacramental bond of unity existing among all who through it are reborn."[16] In practice, however, this incorporation "into Christ and his Church" is experienced "in a given Church or ecclesial Community."[17] In spite of the evident difficulties this presents for the visible unity of Christians in that it hinders "full ecclesial communion," those who "by baptism are incorporated into Christ share many elements of the Christian life. There thus exists a real, even if imperfect, communion among Christians which can be expressed in many ways, including sharing in prayer and liturgical worship . . . . (*UR* 3; 8; 16)."[18]

3.4.1. *The Ecumenical Calling of the Renewal*

The Renewal has been marked for Catholic Christians as well as for "separated brothers and sisters" in Christ by a deep sense of

[16] *Directory for the Application of Principles and Norms on Ecumenism*, 92.
[17] *Ibid.*, 97.
[18] *Ibid.*, 104.

commonality in the experience of "Baptism in the Holy Spirit."
Speaking to leaders of the Renewal, Pope John Paul II stated: "By
your experience of the many gifts of the Holy Spirit which are
shared also with our separated brothers and sisters, yours is the
special joy of growing in a desire for the unity to which the Spirit
guides us and in a commitment to the serious task of ecumenism."[19] Longing and zeal for the unity of Christians is an authentic fruit of the Spirit, who gathers into one: Christians of various
tongues, peoples, cultures and traditions without destroying their
beautiful and mutually beneficial diversity. Catholics in the
Renewal are encouraged to pray and work for the unity of all the
baptized. In doing so they must learn to respect the identity and
diversity of other ecclesial groups and at the same time maintain
their own specific Catholic identity.

While all who are open to the working of the Holy Spirit long
for communion in the true faith, this is not alone a human en-
deavor but ultimately the gift of God. "For this gift of God has
been entrusted to the Church, as breath was to the first created
man, for this purpose, that all the members receiving it may be
vivified; and the [means of] communication with Christ has been
distributed throughout it, that is, the Holy Spirit . . . ."[20] This is a
call to work for unity, a call which demands openness, humility
and prayer.

The Holy Spirit helps us to discover "significant elements" that
"exist outside the visible boundaries of the Catholic Church";
among these are especially the "interior gifts of the Holy Spirit"
experienced in the Renewal (cf. *UR* 3). These must be gratefully
seen as a significant impulse for the unity of Christians. The
Catholic Church encourages whatever draws Christians of the
Renewal closer to their brothers and sisters in other ecclesial bodies: prayer, apostolic zeal for the preaching of the Gospel and,
above all, personal holiness. The Church cannot, however, recognize as fruitful or truly ecumenical an attitude through which
Catholic identity is compromised, limited, or lost.

[19] Pope John Paul II, Address to the Leaders of the Catholic Charismatic Renewal,
May 7, 1981, *Insegnamenti di Giovanni Paolo II*, IV, 1 (Vatican City: Libreria Editrice
Vaticana, 1981) 1126.
[20] Irenaeus of Lyon, *Adversus haereses* 3, 24,1; SCh 211:472.

One important element of this call of the Church for ecumenical encounter is the call for Christians of different persuasions to pray together. This need for prayer among Christians is evident. It must be remembered, however, that prayer is always an expression of the faith and tradition of the Church. It does not occur in an ecumenical vacuum in which the traditions of the various ecclesial bodies are excluded. It may, therefore, occur at times that, when Christians pray regularly together, doctrinal differences surface that tend toward disunity. Differences are often experienced in such questions as the intercession of Mary, the communion of the saints, or even with regard to the interpretation of the Scriptures.[21] When such differences are experienced, it is a part of the call to ecumenism that Christians of different persuasions exercise tolerance and respect for positions they may not understand or be able to accept themselves. Catholics participating in ecumenical prayer groups and communities need to seek appropriate pastoral guidance in order to ensure the maintenance of their Catholic identity. The urgency and experienced need to pray together cannot, however, lead to an ecumenism of purely vague shared feelings that lack a firm foundation in ecclesial tradition.

The Renewal has often helped Catholics to rediscover aspects of their own tradition which they had forgotten and, in doing so, has helped them experience a new respect for their Orthodox, Anglican, Protestant, Pentecostal and non-denominational brothers and sisters. This discovery, however, should not lead to an ecumenical relativism or reductionism in which a few fundamental elements that can be held in common are emphasized to the exclusion of others, which are important and central for the Catholic faith. The celebration of the Sacraments and the explanation of their meaning, the reading and understanding of the Holy Scriptures in the context of the Tradition of the Church, the role of the Mother of God in salvation history, and the intercession of the saints are all fundamental to the faith expressed and experienced in Catholic Tradition. To neglect these aspects of the faith would not only be detrimental to the faith and life of the Church; it would also not

---

[21] This can include also the meaning of pardon and sin, as well as the concepts of redemption and of eternal life.

contribute to a truly ecumenical discovery of the treasures the Catholic Church has to offer. It would be paradoxical when a misconceived ecumenical effort to achieve unity caused new divisions in the Church. No Christian unity can be achieved at the expense of truth, even in areas that have been cause for controversy in the past.

The Catholic faith, properly understood, is an organic whole. While there is a hierarchy of truths, in which some elements are more essential or important, the parts are related to each other in such a way that no part is unimportant or even dispensable. Separating Scripture from Tradition, the charisms from the hierarchical and sacramental structure of the Church, prayer from apostolic witness, conversion from initiation into the concrete communion of God's people would not only be unorganic, it would lead to a concept of the Lordship of Christ that would separate Him from His Body, the Church. It should be noted that St. Paul was very insistent that Christ is not divided (cf. 1 Cor 1:13).

Catholics must be concerned in their ecumenical contacts that they maintain a clear concept of the Doctrine of the Church. There is in some circles a kind of "branch theory" in which the Church, founded by Jesus Christ through His Apostles, exists today in various Christian "denominations," each of which—the Catholic Church included—has its own strengths and weaknesses. This concept would compromise Catholic identity.[22] The Church does not understand herself as a denomination among others.[23] "In fact, the fullness of the unity of the Church of Christ has been maintained within the Catholic Church while other Churches and ecclesial Communities, though not in full communion with the Catholic Church, retain a certain communion with

---

[22] "Catholics hold the firm conviction that the one Church of Christ subsists in the Catholic Church 'which is governed by the successor of Peter and by the Bishops in communion with him' (LG 8)," *Directory for the Application of Principles and Norms on Ecumenism*, 17.

[23] "The Churches and ecclesial Communities not in full communion with the Catholic Church have by no means been deprived of significance and value in the mystery of salvation, for the Spirit of Christ has not refrained from using them as means of salvation," *Ibid.*, 104.

it. The Council affirms: 'This unity, we believe, subsists in the Catholic Church as something she can never lose . . . .' (*UR* 4)."[24]

In all of these areas, discernment is necessary. It is not easy, in a pluralistic situation, to maintain clear concepts. The fundamental criteria of this discernment in the areas of ecumenism are the same as for the exercise of the charisms: truth and love. "Let the work of drawing near to our separated brethren go on, with much understanding, with much patience, with great love; but without deviating from the true Catholic doctrine."[25]

There are two levels of working for unity. Ecumenism on the grassroots level is that experienced most often in the Renewal. There is also an "official" ecumenism, which exists as a dialogue between the leadership of the various Christian churches and ecclesial communities. Both are authentic parts of ecumenism and complement each other. Ecumenism at the grassroots level must, however, be aware of and sensitive to the official level that gives pastoral direction, so that striving for Christian unity does not become naive and unrealistic. The ecumenical dialogue is not, in fact, simply a matter of private initiative. It is the dialogue of "members of the corporate groups in which they have heard the Gospel, and which each regards as his Church and indeed, God's" (*UR* 1).

Genuine ecumenism, inspired by the Holy Spirit, cannot be the attempt to create a sort of inclusive "Church of the Spirit." Authentic ecumenical effort does not seek to avoid the difficult tasks, such as doctrinal convergence, by rushing to create a kind of "Church of the Spirit" that would be autonomous, separate from the visible Church of Christ.[26] The Church itself is already the "Church of the Spirit" in that, from the beginning, the Spirit of God has been the source of its life and power. The Holy Spirit is intimately involved in the Incarnation, the Body of Christ in His hu-

---

[24] *Ibid.*, 18.

[25] Pope John Paul II, Address to the United States Bishops, October 5, 1979. The Pope was quoting from the hand-written text of the Testament of Pope Paul VI dated June 30, 1965.

[26] Cf. Pope John Paul II, Address to Leaders of the Catholic Charismatic Renewal, May 7, 1981, *Insegnamenti di Giovanni Paolo II*, IV, 1 (Vatican City: Libreria Editrice Vaticana, 1981) 1127.

manity born of the Virgin Mary, in His Eucharistic Body, celebrated by Christians since the earliest days of the Church, and in His Body the Church, which is organically and sacramentally structured.

A further ecumenical contribution of the Renewal is the rediscovery of the Church's roots in Judaism. "Baptism in the Holy Spirit" brings a new sensitivity to the "mystery" of Israel of which the Apostle Paul speaks (cf. Rom 11:25-35). By deepening knowledge and respect for authentic Jewish Tradition, Catholics in the Renewal are contributing to the eschatological return of the Messiah in glory and the reuniting of all of God's covenant people. The Renewal commits itself to prayer and to working in appropriate ways for the conversion of the children of Israel, for "God's gifts and his call are irrevocable" (Rom 11:29).

3.4.2. Ecumenism and the Call to Evangelize

A prime impulse to work for Christian unity is, as the Second Vatican Council states, Christ's call to proclaim the Gospel to every creature (cf. UR 1). This theme is taken up by Pope John Paul II in his Encyclical *Ut Unum sint* (May 25, 1995) when he states: "It is obvious that the lack of unity among Christians contradicts the Truth which Christians have the mission to spread and, consequently, it gravely damages their witness" (*UUS* 98). He refers in this context to the Apostolic Exhortation of Pope Paul VI (cf. *EN*) who writes: "As evangelizers, we must offer Christ's faithful not the image of people divided and separated by unedifying quarrels, but the image of people who are mature in faith and capable of finding a meeting-point beyond the real tensions, thanks to a shared, sincere and disinterested search for truth. Yes, the destiny of evangelization is certainly bound up with the witness of unity given by the Church" (*UUS* 98).

The experience of Catholic Christians in the Renewal reflects this appeal of the popes for unity among Christians for the sake of the witness that Christians are obliged to give. The present situation in the world, not least in traditionally Christian areas, calls strongly for a new and renewed effort of evangelization. The common experience of "Baptism in the Holy Spirit" leads to a common desire to share the Good News with others. For this reason, Catholics as well as non-Catholics, who have experienced a renewed relationship to Jesus Christ in the Holy Spirit, seek to give common witness in the most numerous of ways.

Here again, however, ecumenical encounter brings with it numerous difficulties that must be faced. The call to faith in Christ as Lord and Savior is a mutual witness to our faith in the uniqueness of Jesus Christ and His message. This witness is not only possible but required. At the same time there are also differences between the various ecclesial groups in their understanding of what it means to be "incorporated into Jesus Christ."

The Apostolic Exhortation *Evangelii nuntiandi*, in describing the "Content of Evangelization" declares that preaching must include the search for God through prayer, "but also through communion with the visible sign of the encounter with God which is the Church of Jesus Christ, and this communion in its turn is expressed by the application of those other signs of Christ living and acting in the Church which are the Sacraments . . . . In fact, evangelization—over and above the preaching of a message—consists in the implantation of the Church which does not exist without the driving force which is the sacramental life culminating in the Eucharist" (*EN* 28). In arousing, supporting and educating to an acceptance of the need to evangelize, it must be clear that the goal of evangelization "cannot remain abstract and unincarnated, but reveals itself concretely by a visible entry into a community of believers. Thus those whose life is transformed enter a community which is in itself a sign of transformation, a sign of newness of life: the Church is the visible sacrament of salvation" (*EN* 23). The determination of concrete forms of ecumenical collaboration in evangelization cannot therefore be put in an ecclesial context that goes "beyond any denomination" or that is "non-denominational," and which is linked by certain supposed "common roots" or—as in the case of the ecumenical collaboration within the charismatic movement—by a "charismatic identity," understood as a sort of "basic confession," lived variously in individual Churches or ecclesial groups.

This need is not to be perceived as a negative delineation toward other ecclesial groups or as an uncritical and unnecessary continuation of disunity among Christians, but as a part of the needed respect for the differences that do still exist between Christians of various traditions.

The tension between the experienced need to give common witness to the Gospel message and the limitations set by the differences arising from the continuing disunity among Christians is a call to prayer and to a search for an ever broader commonality in truth. The Charismatic Renewal offers much common ground for this process. Cooperation on every possible level, combined with a respect for the integrity of each ecclesial body with its specific traditions, which are often not held in common, needs common prayer and continual conversion in search of God's guidance through the leading of the Holy Spirit. Catholic Christians will always seek the pastoral wisdom of the Church in this pursuit.

CONCLUSION

The Charismatic Renewal sees itself as a work of the Holy Spirit responding to the spiritual needs of our time. It is a sign in the life of the Church of the continuing relevance of the "Outpouring of the Holy Spirit" on the baptized, which gives life and direction to the Church in the accomplishment of its mission in the world. Repeatedly, even prior to the appearance of the Catholic Renewal on the scene, the call for a new Pentecost could be heard. Pope John XXIII asked all the faithful to pray for a new pentecostal "Outpouring of the Holy Spirit" in preparation for the Second Vatican Council.[1] Several years later, reflecting on the experience of the Council, Pope Paul VI exclaimed in a magnificent and prophetic exhortation: "More than once we have asked ourselves what the greatest needs of the Church are, . . . what is the primary and ulti-mate need of our beloved and holy Church? We must say it with holy fear because, as you know, this concerns the mystery of the Church, her life: This need is the Spirit, . . . the Church needs her eternal Pentecost; she needs fire in her heart, words on her lips, a glance that is prophetic."[2] He repeated this theme in an article in *L'Osservatore Romano*: "More than ever, the Church and the world need the miracle of Pentecost to be continued in history."[3] And again, on the occasion of the First International Congress of the Charismatic Renewal held in Rome on Pentecost 1975, he stated: "Nothing is more necessary for an increasingly secularized world,

---

[1] "Renew your wonders in our time, as for a new Pentecost. Grant to Holy Church, united in one insistent and persevering prayer with Mary, the Mother of Jesus, under the guidance of St. Peter, an extension of the kingdom of the divine Saviour, kingdom of truth and justice, of love and peace. Amen."

[2] Pope Paul VI, General Audience, November 29, 1972.

[3] Pope Paul VI, *L'Osservatore Romano*, October 17, 1974.

where God has become a stranger, than the witness of this 'spiritual renewal' which we see the Holy Spirit stirring up today in the most diverse regions and environments."[4]

The Charismatic Renewal has, of course, no monopoly on this renewal for which the popes prayed. There are devoted Catholics around the world who, personally and in their communities, without having any formal connection with the Renewal are clearly open to the guidance and working of the Holy Spirit and are making their profound contribution to this renewal of the Church.

The most profound signs of this renewal of Christ's Church are holiness and evangelization. These are fruits of the working of the Holy Spirit in the world today. The Holy Spirit gives gifts to the children of God, so that they might be more effective witnesses and tools in God's hand for the accomplishment of the Church's mission. The world needs saintly witnesses, whose lives proclaim the reality of what they say. The Renewal should be the school for many such saints in every part of the world and in every circumstance of human society. "Men and women saints have always been the source and origin of renewal in the most difficult circumstances in the Church's history. Today we have the greatest need of saints whom we must assiduously beg God to raise up" (CL 16). During the memorable youth pilgrimage to the Shrine of St. James of Compostela (August 19, 1989) the Holy Father called to the gathered Christian youth: "Do not be afraid to become saints!"

The Church needs men and women in the Renewal to develop fully their baptismal vocation through an intense and pure interior life, giving witness to their union with God and to Jesus Christ in the Holy Spirit. This baptismal vocation of holiness demands "the primacy of life in the Spirit, upon which depends docility to the word, interior prayer, awareness of life as a member of the whole body, desire for unity, dutiful accomplishment of one's official mission, the gift of self in service and the humility of repentance" (Mutuae relationes 4).

---

[4] Pope Paul VI, Pentecost Monday, May 19, 1975.

The various communities, like the individual members of the Renewal, "guided by Him [the Holy Spirit] as the decisive inspirer" (*EN* 75), must become a sign and continuing incentive for the urgency of the Church's apostolate and commission to evangelize. The rich fruits of their missionary zeal, which arise from their obedience to the Holy Spirit and to the Church, are an indication that evangelization does not find its effectiveness in programs, strategies, or techniques, as wise and useful as these may be. The fruits of evangelism grow, as the Acts of the Apostles shows by many examples, out of powerful impulses from the Holy Spirit as they are experienced in obedience to the Community of Faith, the Church.

The Renewal, then, is the servant of Jesus Christ and of His Church. Out of the Church arise ever new saints, who, filled with the inexhaustible energy of the Holy Spirit, fulfill in their lives the mystery of Christ, preparing and hastening the blessed hope of His coming in glory. The Renewal is an instrument of the Holy Spirit in this work, which freely answers her Lord's call: "The Spirit and the Bride say, 'Come!'" (Rev 22:17).

ABBREVIATIONS USED IN THIS WORK

AA	Vatican II	*Apostolicam actuositatem*
AAS		*Acta Apostolica Sedis*
AG	Vatican II	*Ad gentes*
CC		*Corpus Christianorum*
CL	John Paul II	*Christifideles laici*
CT	John Paul II	*Catechesi tradendae*
DV	Vatican II	*Dei verbum*
DEV	John Paul II	*Dominum et vivificantem*
EN	Paul VI	*Evangelii nuntiandi*
FC	John Paul II	*Familiaris consortio*
GS	Vatican II	*Gaudium et spes*
LG	Vatican II	*Lumen gentium*
MD	John Paul II	*Mulieris dignitatem*
PG		*Patrologia graeca*
PO	Vatican II	*Presbyterorum ordinis*
SC	Vatican II	*Sacrosanctum concilium*
SCh		*Sources chrétiennes*
UR	Vatican II	*Unitatis redintegratio*
UUS	John Paul II	*Ut Unum sint*